S0-EIG-592

A CORPORATE REFUGEE
# BARES ALL

# A CORPORATE REFUGEE
# **BARES ALL**

CHALLENGES FACED ... LESSONS LEARNED

## FRANK FREEDMAN
ILLUSTRATED BY ROBB MILLER

MILL CITY PRESS

Mill City Press, Inc.
2301 Lucien Way #415
Maitland, FL 32751
407.339.4217
www.millcitypress.net

© 2018 by Frank Freedman

All rights reserved. No part of this publication may be
reproduced, stored in a retrieval system, or transmitted,
in any form or by any means, electronic, mechanical,
photocopying, recording, or otherwise, without the
prior written permission of the author.

Printed in the United States of America

ISBN-13: 978-1-54562-453-1

I dedicate this book to my mother for her guiding wisdom and to my father for teaching me the nuts and bolts of dealing with people. I also dedicate this book to my thesis advisor Jack Johnson who guided me to learn the underlying tools of my trade. Finally, I dedicate this book to Robert Arthur and Nick Wartonick. These bosses helped me develop professionally by strongly supporting me as I journeyed through uncharted waters.

# Table of Contents

INTRODUCTION . . . . . . . . . . . . . . . . . . . . . . 1

Part One: SciMed Life Systems, Inc. 1969-1976 . . . . 5
  How It All Started. . . . . . . . . . . . . . . . . . . . . .7
  Camaraderie. . . . . . . . . . . . . . . . . . . . . . . .11
  Count Your Blessings. . . . . . . . . . . . . . . . . .14
  How the First Case Went. . . . . . . . . . . . . . . .17
  I Found You a Great Patient . . . . . . . . . . . .21
  Did I Fail God? . . . . . . . . . . . . . . . . . . . . .24
  In Uncharted Waters. . . . . . . . . . . . . . . . . 30
  What an Unusual Day. . . . . . . . . . . . . . . . .33
  The Pending Impeachment . . . . . . . . . . . . .36
  The Purchase Order Is Wrong . . . . . . . . . . .38
  Window of Time. . . . . . . . . . . . . . . . . . . . 41
  Oops . . . . . . . . . . . . . . . . . . . . . . . . . . .44
  I Should Have Told You . . . . . . . . . . . . . . .46
  A Great VA Story . . . . . . . . . . . . . . . . . . .48
  Breath of Life . . . . . . . . . . . . . . . . . . . . . .52
  I Screwed Up. . . . . . . . . . . . . . . . . . . . . . 57
  Before There Was GPS . . . . . . . . . . . . . . . 60
  Colored Tags. . . . . . . . . . . . . . . . . . . . . .62
  Saturday Mornings. . . . . . . . . . . . . . . . . . .64
  "What the Hell Is Going On?" . . . . . . . . . . .65
  Toward Profitability . . . . . . . . . . . . . . . . . .68
  A Memorable Open-Heart Surgery Case. . . . . .72

AFTERWORD . . . . . . . . . . . . . . . . . . . . . . .77

Part Two: Medtronic Inc. 1976-1983. . . . . . . . . . .81
  Here's What I'd Do . . . . . . . . . . . . . . . . . .83
  No Thanks Needed . . . . . . . . . . . . . . . . . .86
  Don't Say Anything. . . . . . . . . . . . . . . . . . .89
  Bittersweet Successes . . . . . . . . . . . . . . . . .91

Please Don't Come Any More . . . . . . . . . . . . . . .95
Hold Them in Receiving. . . . . . . . . . . . . . . . . 100
The Little Boy Who Didn't Die. . . . . . . . . . . . .103
Timing Is Everything . . . . . . . . . . . . . . . . . . .106
Squeezing Out a Decision. . . . . . . . . . . . . . . .108
Putting a Crack in The Glass Ceiling . . . . . . . 110
A Giant Sequoia Towering Over Me. . . . . . . . .114
The Patients Who Died . . . . . . . . . . . . . . . . .118
Do You Remember Those Cases? . . . . . . . . . . 120
New Type of Vice President. . . . . . . . . . . . . .122
But Daddy . . . . . . . . . . . . . . . . . . . . . . . . . .126
Hallelujah . . . . . . . . . . . . . . . . . . . . . . . . . .127
I Found a Table . . . . . . . . . . . . . . . . . . . . . .129
Accounting Needs a Receipt . . . . . . . . . . . . 130
Before There Was E-Mail and Text Messaging . . 131
This Year Budgeting Will Be Easier . . . . . . . . .133
Don't Do that Again . . . . . . . . . . . . . . . . . . .136
Phantom of the Second Floor . . . . . . . . . . . .138
I'll Give You a Ride. . . . . . . . . . . . . . . . . . . .139
Those Small Signs Are Important. . . . . . . . . .141
Corporate Blinders . . . . . . . . . . . . . . . . . . . .142
The Beginning of the End. . . . . . . . . . . . . . . .146
Lovers Who Wander. . . . . . . . . . . . . . . . . . .148
Dear IRS . . . . . . . . . . . . . . . . . . . . . . . . . . 150
Corporate Purgatory. . . . . . . . . . . . . . . . . . .152
Corporate Russian Roulette . . . . . . . . . . . . .156

AFTERWORD . . . . . . . . . . . . . . . . . . . . . . . .159

EPILOGUE . . . . . . . . . . . . . . . . . . . . . . . . . .161
Research Annie . . . . . . . . . . . . . . . . . . . . . .163
Crooked Dick. . . . . . . . . . . . . . . . . . . . . . . .165
Leadership. . . . . . . . . . . . . . . . . . . . . . . . . .168
Get Me Two Things . . . . . . . . . . . . . . . . . . .171

ACKNOWLEDGMENTS. . . . . . . . . . . . . . . . . .175

# INTRODUCTION

I wrote this book for anyone dealing with extreme professional challenges. It's about learning from these experiences and getting on with your professional life. If you have ever been anxious about keeping your job, constantly worrying about everything that's not getting done, dealing with a very problematic boss or devastated by being terminated ... so have I. Take heart! In my experience, something unexpected and wonderful might happen once you make a concerted effort to climb out of corporate hell.

I am an expert at dealing with the most extreme professional challenge .... being terminated. My experience is based on being laid off once and fired three times! My days became filled with anxiety, frustration, anger and sleepless nights. Taking a few ounces of wine or vodka often made the difference between getting fitful sleep or no sleep at all. But these unsettling periods were short-lived. Within a few weeks, I was able to put my circumstances into proper perspective and deal with them as characterized by two lines from Frank Sinatra's 1966 up-lifting hit song "That's Life:"

"Each time I find myself flat on my face ... I pick myself up and get back in the race."

The most important lesson I learned and practiced was to get "back in the race" quickly after being fired ... all three times. That allowed me to then focus on finding my next job. Being angry or feeling sorry for myself was a waste of time and emotional energy. Hurtful feelings surfaced from time to time after each firing. But I never let them hinder me from getting on with my professional life. And something good subsequently happened each time.

The second most important lesson was realizing the need to pursue opportunities that luckily arise. The third most important lesson learned was that creativity was far more helpful in overcoming the challenges I faced than all my college courses and leadership training I received. But being creative involves taking a risk and a leap of faith that everything will work out. I was respectful and showed an interest in my fellow employees. Doing so is inherent is my DNA and sometimes unexpectedly paid off big dividends. These and other lessons I learned and practiced are noted throughout this book.

Taking comedy improvisation classes taught me that even the most serious adversities might later be recalled as humorous. If you don't believe me, consider what I told my classmates at our 40th reunion when we were asked to summarize our accomplishments since high school:

> "I was laid off and fired from some of the finest medical device companies in the Twin Cities during 14 years with four companies. My first employer laid me off. That termination led me to become a co-founder of a new company, SciMed Life Systems, Inc. My other three employers fired me. All three subsequently hired me back as a consultant. I consulted at one former company for 14 years, twice the seven years that I was an employee there. In each case, the people who fired me were either

fired, demoted or asked to "retire" within a year. I ultimately started my own consulting business, so I could not be fired any more. A lot of my consulting business came from the three companies that fired me. One former boss who had fired me gave me an unsolicited glowing recommendation to a prospective consulting client."

My professional career always placed me in the forefront of an evolving organization or new technology. That led to many highs and lows in my career, not unlike a roller coaster ride. During my medical device career, I observed the workplace introduction of microelectronics, personal computers, portable pagers, e-mail, smart phones, virtual companies, home-office businesses, text messaging and social media. While I never found my workplace niche, I thoroughly enjoyed the ride.

This book as a collection of interwoven short stories I've told over the years. I am a storyteller who comes from a family of story-tellers. At family gatherings, my father and his two brothers pushed each aside so they could tell the next story. They told endless stories about their youth, past family members and everyday things that happened to them. Most were funny. Some were heart-breaking.

This book is neither an exposé nor a condemnation of the medical device corporate world. I readily acknowledge my companies made many, many positive contributions that saved patients or improved their lives. Rather, my book is about what I experienced and learned when facing agonizing personal and professional adversities sprinkled liberally among some notable successes.

Family values, my father's sense of humor and my mother's wisdom and philosophy guided me in taking actions and making decisions when dealing with adversity. My mother died too early for me to know her much as an adult. But I often recall her urging me to "leave this earth in better shape than you found it." I believe my work on medical devices probably saved hundreds of patients' lives and provided vastly improved treatment results for thousands and thousands of others. Some of my volunteer activities involved helping dozens of former colleagues and strangers find jobs. Readers can judge whether or not I achieved my mother's humble expectation.

# Part One
# SciMed Life Sciences Inc.

# 1969 – 1976

Part One describes my first two jobs in the medical device industry. It is virtually all about my experiences working at a new company that I and five others co-founded.

We planned to develop and provide two life-saving products. Initially, I did not realize that I had embarked upon a career that was like a roller coaster ride. The highs and lows were sometimes too small to notice. Other times, there were substantial ascents relating to huge successes or rapid descents due to spectacular failures.

We worked long, hard hours. SciMed struggled to survive financially while offering two new products to save or improve the lives of patients.

The strong sense of camaraderie at SciMed was my salvation. It gave me comfort and reassurance after many setbacks. Perseverance, a sense of humor and creativity were the tools I used to trouble-shoot and solve problems. There was constant need to bounce back from adversity to stay focused on making SciMed a success.

In the last few years of my tenure there, the highs and lows became more pronounced. Profitability was just around the corner. Right after solving a potential company-ending crisis, I was fired!

# How It All Started

**What I Learned:** Is what I experienced and learned more than twenty-five years ago still relevant in today's corporate world? It certainly is. Being laid off or fired, for example, regardless of the circumstances still sucks!

My first corporate job lasted only 3 months. I joined the Applied Science Division of Litton Industries after leaving my Assistant Professorship at Rose Polytechnical Institute (now Rose Hulman University) in Terre Haute Indiana. While I enjoyed teaching in their bioengineering program, I left for a seemingly better job in the medical device industry. My wife and I were also pleased to be returning with our children to the Minneapolis area in my adopted home state.

My new job was to transform a prototype artificial lung into a fully developed, reliable product that could be used to breathe for acute lung failure patients while their own lungs healed. I really enjoyed working on this product. After six weeks on the job, my wife and I bought our first house. We did so because the General Manager told me our division was doing well and that its future looked "great."

But it was not doing great. It soon shut down, and everyone was laid off but Rollie Gagnon the division's security officer. That made him responsible for the contracts, reports, equipment and other things related to the division's government-sponsored research projects.[1] Therefore, it was not prudent to fire him. Rollie and I and four other former employees decided to purchase the division. Since the country was going through a recession, we knew that finding a job elsewhere would be very difficult for technical people like us. We were allowed to remain in the office to purchase and plan for the new business. It would be called SciMed Life Systems, Inc. SciMed was our Plan A. Given the recession, we had no Plan B.

There was no reception, ribbon-cutting or other celebratory event to launch SciMed. The earliest events I recalled involved was the many times we overheard Rollie negotiating on our behalf to purchase the division with a Litton Industry corporate attorney. The attorney seemed like a short, stocky mobster with a slick hair-cut and dressed in an expensive business suit. Rollie was a tall, lanky man who, in negotiations, acted like a clueless Neanderthal.

The negotiations could be overheard through the thin conference room door and walls. Rollie's approach was to wear the attorney down by acting dumb and making outrageous demands. The attorney hated explaining why so many things Rollie sought were impossible to grant. Negotiations usually involved about five minutes of normal conversation followed by a minute or two

---

[1] This contract research included building prototype Doppler radar units and microwave ovens and developing nerve agent detection kits and two early stage, life-saving medical products ... a new type of Artificial Lung and a Laminar Flow Patient Isolation Room. Previously, this Division had helped develop "Alvin" the first deep-sea diving submarine. Hospitals installed Laminar Flow Rooms to protect vulnerable bone marrow transplant patients from contracting air-borne hospital infections. It gained notoriety a few years later, as the all-encompassing environment in the "Boy in the Bubble" movie. I would be developing the Artificial Lung that could potentially save thousands of lives, by breathing for patients dying from acute lung failure.

of them yelling at each other. We thought Rollie was doing a great job.

One negotiating session we all heard was quite memorable. The tone suddenly changed from yelling to screaming vulgarities at each other. We feared negotiations might abruptly end permanently. But they did not. There was a brief pause when the attorney must have suddenly realized he was negotiating with a fellow Litton Industry employee. He shouted out at the top of his lungs, "You're fired!"

After another pause, the negotiations continued as though nothing out of the ordinary had happened. The five of us looked at each other. Did we really hear what we just heard? We all broke out in hysterical yet muted laughter, since we did not want the attorney to know that we could hear everything. A day or so later, negotiations were successfully concluded. SciMed would become a reality.

This story depicts my first professional career roller coaster ride. The "high" of getting a seemingly great job at Litton Industries was short-lived. Unexpectedly, the ride accelerated downward to the "low" of being terminated. It was really scary being terminated. My wife and I had just used all of our savings to buy a house and move our furniture from Terre Haute into it. What if we co=founders were not able to buy the Applied Science Division? What if we could not raise the money needed to fund SciMed's operations? If we failed, the likelihood of any of us quickly finding another job was bleak. I felt helpless. I had absolutely no answer to my wife's simple question. "What are we going to do?"

But my ride then headed upward. We were able to purchase the division's assets on favorable terms and raise money to fund SciMed. I envisioned a bright medical device industry career ahead and a good investment return for being a SciMed co-founder and investor.

Was I qualified to assume any of the responsibilities that I would assume at SciMed? Not really.

# Camaraderie

**What I Learned:** *There is a difference between colleagues and friends. Both can be supportive when you need it most. But only your friends will show up at your funeral.*

I t was not a pretty place, nor even a relaxing one. Rather, it was just a long table and folding chairs in a factory setting near the rear of the SciMed Life Systems building. But something wonderful happened every time we sat there to have our morning coffee break. At first, I did not quite understand what I was observing while listening to the warm and friendly conversations.

I had never observed such camaraderie among colleagues, as I did when I sat there with the twelve or so other ex-Litton employees during coffee breaks and lunch. As the newcomer, I mostly listened to their conversations. They talked about their families, their dreams and their problems. I could tell that they truly cared for each other. They were committed to make our fledgling young company a success. Sometimes we even had a little fun with each other.

Ed came out of retirement to rejoin his former Litton Industry colleagues at SciMed. Retirement was not for him. I remember him as an easy going, jovial skilled machinist. Silver-haired and stocky in build, he always had a smile on his face. He could operate every piece of equipment in our machine shop. During one coffee break, we kidded Ed about buying a large, luxurious car. When asked why he bought it, his response was that "it gets great gas mileage." But we suspected that he felt awkward about spending some of his retirement money to buy a luxurious car and really didn't know the gas mileage he got. The next day at coffee someone brought the subject up again. When Ed repeated his claim about great gas mileage, he was asked to measure it and let us know. He had no idea we planned to add gasoline back into his car's tank several times during the ensuing days.

About a week later. acknowledging his own disbelief, Ed exclaimed, "I get almost 80 miles a gallon!" Naturally, we expressed our disbelief too. We teased him for a few minutes about how improbable that was. So someone asked him to measure it again. He agreed. During the next few days, we took turns siphoning gas from his car's gas tank. A few days later Ed reluctantly stated, "It gets only 5 miles per gallon. I guess I was wrong." The true mileage was never established, nor did it really matter.

As my workload increased, I had less time for coffee breaks. My work required me to make more and more decisions on my own. Neither I nor anyone else had any training or experience to guide these decisions. I always tried to do the right thing. If I was wrong, I could always count on my colleagues' support of the risks I took and their understanding about mistakes I made. Their support and understanding meant the world to me.

Coffee breaks continued as the Company grew. While the camaraderie we had in the early days was never lost, the opportunities to engage others in it slowly dwindled away. There were too many new faces and no table big enough to accommodate everyone. In a way, the advent of the lunch room at SciMed with many small tables was the culprit.

My colleagues supported me and I enjoyed the camaraderie for almost 7 years, until I was fired.

# Count Your Blessings

***What I Learned:*** *It's great to take the initiative. But be sure to "look before you leap."*

I was 30 years old. Life was good ... good family, friends, health and education and a great job. While I had many blessings in my life, I never took even a moment to reflect about how fortunate I was. That changed when I was caught on the wrong side of doing someone a favor.

During one coffee break, a new employee asked for help moving into his new apartment the next Saturday. To make him feel welcomed into the company, three of us eagerly agreed to help. Without thinking, I volunteered to take the U.S. Navy truck we had parked out back to help him move. It was a large old, flat-bed truck that the Navy had loaned to Litton Industries for its nerve agent kit testing. SciMed kept it for the few times it was needed to carry some employees and their equipment to a remote site for nerve agent kit field testing.

Taking the initiative, like borrowing this truck and driving it, was nothing new for me. As a toddler, my mother once put me outside to play. She tied a long rope from a clothes pole to one of my overall straps, thinking I would be safe outside and not wander away while she did housework inside. But I wanted to explore the neighborhood. So, I climbed out of my overalls and went off to explore it.

Saturday morning the three of us met at SciMed. We were unshaven and dressed in old tattered clothing for the move. We looked so ragged that any one seeing us probably would have thought that we were just three bums who hopped off a passing freight train and stole the truck. I drove toward a New Hope (a Minneapolis suburb) address to pick up the furniture that had to be moved.

While we were at a stop sign, a New Hope police cruiser drove up right behind us with its lights flashing.

The police officer walked over to me and asked, "Whose truck is this? It has no license plates."

I was terrified. "Oh my god," I thought. I'm in a lot of trouble." I never asked for permission to take the truck. I could be fired. Even worse, I would have to go to jail. What would I do?"

Using the most authoritarian attitude I could create, I replied, "IT BELONGS TO THE U.S. NAVY."

"OK" he said, "But get a license plate for it."

My companions did not know that I was terrified, or how relieved I was to hear the officer's response. I was very "lucky." After that incident, I stopped taking the blessings that came my way for granted.

I still recall this incident now almost fifty years later, each time I stop at that intersection.

# How the First Case Went

**What I Learned:** *Most of us are not really lucky. Rather, we are smart enough to whole-heartedly pursue those opportunities that luckily arise.*

I started making lists of things I had to do. No matter how many items I could cross off each day, at least a few more were added. Sometimes I would wake up from a fitful sleep, thinking about something else I had to do at work. When this happened, I wrote the new task on a small pad I kept on my night stand and went back to sleep.

Animal studies at several major medical centers indicated that our artificial lung was ready for human use. These studies showed that it was safe to use to "breathe" for patients with severe acute lung failure. It could provide such patients several days or more for their own lungs to heal.[2] Therefore, the number one thing on my list was getting our lung used for a patient.

I visited some of these medical centers. I developed a rapport with key physicians who expressed an interest in using our lung. But nothing I did seemed to work. It

---

[2] Artificial lungs commonly used in heart-lung machines during the 1970's used a diffusing stone to add oxygen to blood, similar to how oxygen is added to an aquarium by bubbling air into it. Our new artificial lung and a few others like it had a membrane imposed between blood flowing on one side of it and oxygen flowing on the other side. Oxygen moved across the membrane into the flowing blood, similar to how it moves across lung cells superimposed between flowing blood and air drawn deep into our lungs. Since membrane lungs were relatively safe to use for several days, physicians could use them to breathe for patients until their own lungs could heal.

17

was frustrating to wait month after month for our lung to get used. My frustration heightened when I learned that competitive artificial lungs were now being used and had saved a few patients dying from acute lung failure.

We anxiously waited for our first case to happen. Was it ever going to happen?

Then one morning a Dr. Woodrow Wilson "Tim" Havens from the Bethesda Naval Hospital called me. Bethesda Naval Hospital is the well-known Washington D.C.-area medical center where Presidents go for their annual physical examination or treatment, as do other dignitaries. I quickly formed a mental picture of him as a young, energetic surgeon who was not afraid of taking the initiative. He joined the U.S. Navy as a Lieutenant JG (junior grade) and was assigned to Bethesda, instead of the Vietnam war zone. Within a few months, he had taken over much of their animal research studies.

Tim was in charge of animal studies evaluating the use of our artificial lung and a competitive model made by a General Electric division. Both could breathe for patients with severe acute lung failure. A sailor was dying of acute lung failure and had an urgent need for an artificial lung. The hospital did not have any artificial lungs, since the ones sold them had all been used in their animal studies. Could we expedite shipping one by air freight? What a great opportunity to have our lung finally used. Without hesitation, I took one from inventory and raced by car to the airport to ship it air express.

We anxiously awaited the results of our first case. Did our lung work? Was a patient saved? Finally, Tim called. I was paged throughout the building, telling me that Dr. Havens from Bethesda Naval was calling.

I felt an adrenaline rush. My heart was pounding as I raced to from the rear of the building to my office to take the call. I heard shouts of encouragement as a raced to my office. Everyone knew it was an important call. We would finally hear about the first case with our artificial lung. By the time I reached my office, a small group of employees had already gathered there to listen to my telephone conversation.

"The lung worked great. The patient didn't live. We didn't expect him to." After telling me some details about the case, Tim asked if I wanted to know how our artificial lung got used. Naturally, I did.

"My immediate superior wanted to use General Electric's lung since it had been used for several cases elsewhere. I wanted to use yours; it worked well and was easier to use. So we went up the hospital's chain of command to seek a decision from the surgical administrator about which lung to use. This officer's decision was to order both artificial lungs. The first one to arrive would be used for this case.

"I really wanted to use your lung for our first case," he said. He explained how he made that happen.

"I sent a corpsman in a Jeep to Dulles Airport to pick up the General Electric lung, shipped to D.C. from Milwaukee. Another corpsman and I took an ambulance to National (now Reagan National) Airport to pick up your lung, shipped in from Minneapolis. We turned on the ambulance sirens and flashing lights so we could race to the airport at high speeds. I even got permission to drive onto the tarmac, right up to the taxied plane. Your lung was the first thing taken from the cargo hold. We raced back to the hospital and beat the corpsman in the jeep by over a half hour. That's how your lung got to be used for the patient."

That experience was a roller coaster ride. There was the "high" of having our lung work well during its first use. It was immediately followed by the "low" of learning that the patient died. His acute lung failure was too severe for his lungs to heal. The ride back down was cushioned by recalling the absurd way our lung got to be used. I was thankful for Tim's initiative.

# I Found You
# a Great Patient

***What I Learned:*** *Trust your gut. If it tells you some-*
*thing might not be right, then it*
*may be wrong.*

While in the Washington D.C. area shortly after
this first case, I decided to visit Bethesda Naval
Hospital. Besides giving technical advice to physicians,
it was my job to sell our artificial lungs. Although I
dreaded having to sell anything, I thought it might be
easy to sell some to Bethesda. I would simply ask if
they wanted to buy a few artificial lungs to have some
in stock for their next case.

The surgical administrator was glad to meet with
me. He was a middle-aged, career U.S. Navy officer,
neatly attired in his naval officer's dress uniform. His
office had a clean, crisp appearance, like a sterile operating room before a case began. Everything was organized and in its place. From his tone and demeanor, he
struck me as a good administrator ... politically wise
and dedicated to keeping his department running well
and on course. Our conversation was mildly interesting,
until he expressed his pleasure about how well their
first case went.

"Frank," he said "I've been thinking about that case
and our situations. What we really both need is for us
to use your lung to save a dignitary .... a U.S. Senator,
maybe an ambassador. Wouldn't it be great, if we saved
someone like that?" Was he sincere or just boasting?

While I was not actively looking for any dignitary or high-ranking government official in acute lung failure to treat, one surfaced in newspaper and television stories a few months later. I wrestled in my mind about calling the surgical administrator.

Would he accept my suggesting a prominent patient as helpful? Or, would he view me as a "smart ass" who called him out on an insincere suggestion. After some thought, I decided to call him.

After we exchanged greetings, I quietly stated that "I found the exact patient you are looking for. He's 79 years old and dying from pneumonia (a common type of acute lung failure). While he lives in Missouri, I assume you have the authority to commandeer a respiratory support team and Navy cargo plane to fly him back for treatment. His last name is Truman … President Harry S. Truman."

He took a few moments to think. "Oh no" he exclaimed. "We could not do that. If he died under our care, it would kill our research programs."

I immediately realized that my suggestion had crossed the line. Silly me thinking that an administrator would take such a chance. I was too embarrassed to tell anyone at SciMed about this incident. I swallowed hard and accepted this "low." But like that line in Sinatra's song, I quickly got "back into the race" and charged ahead toward my goal of making SciMed successful.

Bethesda Naval Hospital never did another case or even order any more lungs from us. But it played a major role in SciMed's future. Bethesda's research programs trained other Navy physicians how to use our artificial lung. They used it successfully elsewhere at places like Johns Hopkins and Massachusetts General Hospitals after their discharge from the Navy.

This incident should have taught me to tune into my instincts. I knew there was a risk in suggesting President Truman as a good candidate … but I ignored it.

# Did I
# Fail God?

***What I Learned:*** *Things happen for a reason, like being in the right place at the right time.*

G ood news can arise when least expected. After a year of clinical experience with our artificial lung, there were but a handful of survivors. SciMed was only selling a few artificial lungs each week ... far too few to stem the flow of red ink that poured across the company's financial records.

An unexpected announcement by the National Institutes of Health (NIH) might change that. NIH announced funding for a large research study. The study's purpose was to learn which types of acute lung failure could heal, if an artificial lung was used to keep patients alive while their lungs healed. We were pleased to learn that most physician researchers in this pending NIH study would be using our artificial lung. If this study was successful, it was possible that other physicians might start using our product. Not a roller coaster high ... just a little ride up!

Humanity is far from its finest when impatient passengers rush to board an airplane. They push and shove each other as they plod ahead toward their assigned seat. It is never as simple as just walking unimpeded toward your seat. By row 14, you notice that a few passengers are heading toward you. They are frantically searching for any open overhead bin to store their baggage and coats. A flight attendant and an angry passenger temporarily block your movement past row 19, as they try to determine who really belongs in seat B. Two unruly, screaming children sitting next to their frazzled mother in row 22 could set the stage for a long, unpleasant flight.

I was one of those impatient passengers boarding an airplane early one Friday evening. It had been another week of traveling. I was glad to be going home. No doubt I pushed or shoved a fellow passenger or two while boarding. If I did, it was to find an open seat next to someone who might be interesting to talk with. I was married but not dead. That's why I also looked to sit next to an attractive woman that I could possibly flirt with ... but just a little.

I spotted an empty seat next to an attractive, young brunette. She was stunning ... perfect hair ... great make up ... and possibly even interesting to chat with as well. I quickly took it instead of my assigned seat.

She smiled at me as I sat down. I started a conversation by asking, "Are you going to Minneapolis for business or pleasure?"

She immediately began to cry. In between deep sobs she said, "My mother is dying. She can't breathe. They called me to come as soon as possible." Emotionally, she was a wreck. I sensed a mixture of fear, anxiety and uncertainty.

Her mother was at a prestigious Minnesota medical center for routine surgery. But she vomited during surgery and was having trouble breathing. I quickly realized that her mother probably had aspiration pneumonia, a rare surgical complication. It occurs when the anesthetic makes a patient nauseous. The nausea can be severe enough to cause vomiting. When it does, each time the patient inhales to take in another breath vomitus is drawn deep into their lungs. That blocks the airways, and breathing becomes extremely difficult. Her mother was mostly likely drowning in her own vomitus. Her routine surgery had turned into an emergency.

"If this woman has aspiration pneumonia and is dying," I wondered, "did God put me next to her daughter in this plane?" I was only one of several dozen people worldwide who knew that our type of artificial lung could treat this type of acute lung failure. Without any hesitation, I offered to help when we got to Minneapolis. So much for flirting or having an interesting conversation.

I called the medical center's nursing station, when we arrived at the airport. My grateful but anxious fellow passenger was by my side. "This is Dr. Freedman," I boldly announced. "I'm at the Minneapolis Airport with a daughter of one of your patients" whom I named. That immediately got the attending physician on the line. "Is she in acute lung failure? Is she dying?" I asked.

"No. She is not dying, nor is she in acute lung failure," was the response. Thinking I was a physician, the doctor told me, "It is a cardiac problem, and her condition has been stabilized."

I explained that the daughter was told her mother was dying due to breathing problems just a few hours ago. "If that is the case," I said, "I may be able help. I'm a biomedical engineer working on an artificial lung to breathe for patients with acute lung failure. I could possibly get help from a University of Minnesota surgical team to come to your hospital and place this patient on our artificial lung."

I knew that the university's surgical team was skilled at operating a bedside-version of a heart-lung machine that used our artificial lung to breathe for patients with severe acute lung failure. If they agreed, and her mother was dying of aspiration pneumonia, their help could save her.

"That is not the case" I was told. "We are treating her for a cardiac condition and she is stable." Great news, I thought. I thanked her and ended the telephone call.

I told the daughter that her mother's breathing problems were due to a heart problem. She was stable now. This information was comforting.

It was almost 11:00 pm on this Friday night. I was tired but relieved. I showed her where to get transportation to the medical center treating her mother. As fate would have it, I gave her my telephone number in case she might need it. It turns out that she did.

My wife and I were awakened out of a deep sleep by a frantic 2:00 am telephone call.

"My mother is dying!" the young woman screamed. "She can't breathe!"

I reiterated my earlier explanation about her mother's condition and that I could not help her. She hung up on me. I felt helpless and could imagine her frustration and anger.

While waiting in the Minneapolis Airport three days later, I decided out of curiosity to call about this patient. I again called as "Dr. Freedman" and learned that she died of acute lung failure. I was stunned!

Did this prestigious medical center purposely give me erroneous information about a patient? Or did doctors there simply not know how to distinguish acute lung failure from an acute cardiac condition? Admittedly, the clinical signs and symptoms for both conditions are very similar. Maybe they just did not want any outside help, since that would have meant that they did not know how to treat this patient.

It was a very unsettling introduction to the imperfect practice of medicine ... a definite "low" for me. I had a chance to save a life. My unbridled enthusiasm to help save lives had to give way to reality. I had been visiting physicians using our lung and others who might consider using it for more than two years. Yet wide-spread acceptance of our artificial lung as a promising new therapy was still an elusive goal. There was nothing major I could directly do to make a huge difference. Baby steps would have to suffice.

Reluctantly, I had to accept that life-threatening acute lung failure can sometimes be improperly diagnosed as a heart problem. One deadly form of acute lung failure is still often only diagnosed by autopsy!

To this day, I still think God put me next to this woman on that plane. If so, did I somehow fail to act on the rest of God's plan for me to help save her mother.

# In Uncharted Waters

**What I Learned:** *Taking a risk involves a leap of faith that everything will work out ok.*

There is a saying about "not being afraid to go outside of your comfort zone." I do not know any saying about how uncomfortable that could be. As an academically trained biomedical engineer, I had the technical expertise but not the skills needed to sell our artificial lung for acute respiratory failure. But I had to sell this product. The company desperately needed the cash that more sales could provide.

Plenty of surgeons called to ask about using our artificial lung on acute lung failure patients. I was always able to answer their technical and clinical questions. Some surgeons invited me to demonstrate how to set up and use our lung at their facility. But SciMed's tight finances only allowed me to accept a small number of invitations to conduct on-site demonstrations. I had to be careful about which invitations to accept, since the company was far from profitable.

One day a Detroit surgeon from Henry Ford Hospital called to invite me to demonstrate our product. He told me his plans to conduct animal research to train his heart-lung technicians to use our artificial lung. I found him to be easy going, well-informed and far more invested in using our lung than most surgeons.

I sensed a golden opportunity to sell some product. Without hesitation, I told him: "Doctor, we are a small start-up company. It's important that cash cross our palms quickly, if I agree to come there." To my delight, he agreed.

I entered Henry Ford Hospital through the emergency room entrance. It looked like an Army MASH Unit, in the midst of an urban battlefield. Serious accident and assault victims were everywhere. Several armed security guards kept a watchful eye on everyone there. Once the reason for my visit was confirmed, I was given a pass to the third floor. The surgeon would meet me at the elevator. I was told not to go anywhere in that hospital without my pass and an escort.

I remember the surgeon only as a personable professional in green surgical scrubs who had a receding hairline. As we walked, he told me they had no animal research facility and could not perform animal research in any operating room. I was led to what appeared to be a rarely used, out-of-the-way maintenance area. He had set it up as a temporary animal surgical area where I could train his heart-lung machine team. They were easy to train. Once anesthetized, a large dog was connected to their heart-lung machine with our lung in it. It worked well for the hour or two it was used.

The dog recovered very quickly. The team found our lung easy to use. The surgeon was pleased!

The surgeon and I talked for about 30 minutes after the case. That is how long it took to work up enough courage to ask him to buy a small inventory of products. I took a risk. It worked ... my first sale to a physician not already using our artificial lung. This sale changed everything. I would no longer be swimming frantically in uncharted waters, wallowing in my hesitancy to ask for a sale. To this day, I rarely hesitate to ask for something that makes sense to me. A few times though, doing so caused far more work or unforeseen problems for me to tackle than I had envisioned before asking.

# What an Unusual Day

**What I Learned:** *Every day is "Curtain Up" with you starring in a comedy, tragedy, adventure or something else.*

I looked forward to visiting Johns Hopkins Hospital to meet with Dr. Jack White. He had used a small version of our artificial lung to save a few tiny premature babies dying from hyaline membrane disease, a life-threatening condition due to their undeveloped lungs. Jack gained national notoriety in medical circles for this extraordinary accomplishment. I was thrilled that he was willing to meet with me.

We had a great conversation, easy-going and informative. He was an intelligent, dedicated physician. This tall, handsome man easily could have passed as a movie star. I thanked Jack for setting up a meeting for me with one of the hospital's senior heart-lung technicians.

I hoped Jack's experience with our artificial lung and his introduction might help me convince this technician to use our lung in their longer, more complex open-heart surgery procedures. By this time, SciMed realized that acute lung failure would not be a major market. Artificial lung use in open-heart surgery would, instead, be the key to the company's profitability and future. Meeting this technician at such a prestigious hospital was a very big deal!

The technician was a stocky man dressed in his surgical scrubs and surrounded in his office by numerous

open-heart surgical devices. Those devices were props
he used to proclaim himself a "leading open-heart technical authority." He was not shy about telling me how
great his professional accomplishments were.

I had to wait to ask about using our lung in open
heart surgery cases until he finished boasting about his
technical accomplishments, published research arti-
cles and familiarity with our artificial lung. He readily
agreed with my contention that our artificial lung might
be safer to use in some of their open-heart surgical
cases than their current artificial lungs. Before I could
process this good news came the bad news. He made
it very clear that would only happen if he got a substantial "monetary reward" for each unit used at Johns
Hopkins Hospital.

One of my mother's guiding principles was that
"honesty was always the best policy." Giving someone
a kick-back for product sales was against my principles.
I told my boss Art Anderson about this conversation.
I was glad to learn that he shared my values. SciMed
would not offer a kick-back for product use. It was devastating to have come so close to a sale at a prestigious
hospital. But this decision was the right one.

My flight home took me from a mild sunny Baltimore
winter day to a dark, cold, sub-zero Minnesota night.
Howling frigid winds whistled by me as I walked
through the airport parking lot searching for my car. It
was so cold that I could hear the frozen snow-covered
ground crack sharply with each step I took. I looked and
looked for my car while dragging a lot of heavy things
back home from this week's trip. I had more than just
my luggage and briefcase with me. Since liquor taxes
were so low in Baltimore, I was also dragging empty

artificial lung cartons filled with less expensive wine and liquor bought in Baltimore.

"Where did I park the damn car?" I was tired and freezing. I could barely recall what cities I had visited that week, let alone where I parked my car a few days earlier. Once I woke up in my airport motel room one morning not knowing what city I was in. There were so many trips. My young kids just thought I went to the airport every Monday, stayed there for a few days and then came home.

After almost 30 minutes of searching, I suddenly realized that I didn't drive to the airport. It was too cold to do so; my car battery would have been dead by the time I arrived back in Minneapolis. I finally remembered that I took a taxi to the airport and would need to take one home.

What a day it had been ... confronted with a serious ethical dilemma followed by exposure to freezing weather conditions due to forgetfulness on my part.

# The Pending Impeachment

***What I Learned:*** *Teaching right from wrong does not just apply to parenting.*

I occasionally strike up a conversation with an interesting-looking stranger. It was a trait I learned as a teenager watching my father talk to old and new customers in his store. Sometimes just asking how someone's day was going would lead to the most interesting conversation. A chance encounter while standing in an airport line to check in for a flight provided a great reason to start a conversation.

Our nation at the time was both fascinated and disgusted with the on-going "Watergate Scandal." It had been front page news or the lead-off television news story for many months. Having followed the televised Senate hearings, I recognized the tall, stately and impeccably dressed gentleman in a business suit standing in front of me. It was Wisconsin U.S. Senator William Proxmire, a ranking member of the Senate Watergate Committee.

I asked if he would mind me telling him what I thought about the hearings. Presumably he did not want to say yes. But how could he really say no? His demeanor as he turned to listen suggested that he was bracing to hear criticism, anger or some marginally useful suggestion. It would not be anything good.

"Senator, my oldest daughter is six years old. She has seen some Watergate news stories and your committee hearings on television about President Nixon. Recently, she asked me 'Was President Nixon bad?' When I told her I thought so, she asked, "Then why is he still President? With the hearings dragging on so long, that's been a tough question that many parents have been struggling to answer."

"It looks like Nixon will be forced to resign. If he does resign, it will be a great example for parents trying to teach their children right from wrong."

He smiled and wished me a safe trip. I suspected that he was relieved to hear something positive about Watergate.

# The Purchase Order Is Wrong

***What I Learned:*** *Instincts have been used since the dawn of time to size up situations. Early cave men grabbed their hunting tools, when they sensed a herd of mammoth thundering by.*

I was excited about visiting Lackland Air Force Hospital, a sprawling medical complex near the Lackland Air Force Base in San Antonio, Texas. A surgical team there had been using our lung in animal studies to learn how to use it in open-heart surgical procedures. I was invited there to observe the last such animal study. While they had been buying one or two artificial lungs every week, I hoped to get a purchase order for their initial open-heart surgery cases.

The animal case went well. Afterwards, the cardiac surgeon told me that he was very satisfied with our product. I readily accepted his invitation to tour the cardiac unit. He was a very congenial, soft-spoken man in whom I saw great inner strength. His neatly groomed uniform proudly showed his rank of colonel.

While touring, we talked about many things both professional and personal. Getting to know this surgeon a little was very enjoyable. I was thrilled to learn the hospital would be ordering our lung to use during upcoming open-heart surgery cases. That would make it the third or fourth hospital in the country to do so. A lot of hard work was starting to pay off.

To get some idea about how many artificial lungs they might order, I asked about their case load. He told me they usually perform four or five open-heart cases a week. Hearing this, I thought that we might get an order for five-ten lungs initially. But he cautioned me not to expect an order for a month or more. Their relatively small cardiac post-operative recovery unit was being remodeled. Until the remodeling was finished, they would only be performing emergency cases.

My boss Art shared my enthusiasm about getting Lackland's next purchase order. When it came about four weeks later, it was for 300 artificial lungs. A purchase order this large was a blessing ... a cause for celebration ... if only it was correct. My instincts told me immediately that it was incorrect, A bizarre picture flashed through my mind. Since the small post-operative recovery unit could only accommodate a few patients, I envisioned dozens of patients recovering in a line of beds extending from that unit, down the hallway, through the main lobby and ending somewhere on the front lawn. Clearly, I had a creative mind that in this case was not rooted in reality.

Reluctantly, I told Art that the purchase order was probably wrong. The only way it could be right would be if Lackland planned to use this large inventory to supply other Air Force hospitals. But this scenario seemed very unlikely. Concerned I might be wrong, Art called the purchasing agent who confirmed that the purchase order was correct. Art was a gentle giant. He was a frustration executive but wonderful scientist who rarely got excited about anything. But he was elated!

The news about such a large order spread quickly at our small, three-year old company. Within hours, everyone at SciMed and our entire Board of Directors knew about this phenomenal achievement. An order this large would help get us to profitability. It was exciting news!

Still instincts told me that the order was wrong. I had to check on the order myself before I could celebrate along with my colleagues.

First, I called the head heart-lung machine technician. In the past, he bought a few lungs weekly only on an emergency basis for their animal research studies. This time he sent a requisition to purchase five lungs for their first few cases. Next, I called the supply sergeant about the order. Since the technicians had been ordering products weekly on an "emergency basis," he decided to increase the order from five to 20. He did that so he, "would not be bothered processing so many emergent purchasing requests."

But ordering 20 products for the first few cases did not explain why 300 artificial lungs were ordered. So

I checked further. Guess what the supply captain did to avoid those weekly "emergency" purchasing requisitions? He increased the order from 20 to 50 units. And the same scenario played out with the purchasing agent who upped the total order from 50 to 300 artificial lungs.

Needless to say, the celebratory mood ceased when the purchase order was cancelled; a new one was issued for far fewer products. But we should have been celebrating this small but important victory. SciMed's pathway to financial success was primarily achieved along a trail of many, many small victories.

# Window of Time

**What I Learned:** *Everyone makes mistakes. Some can be quite spectacular.*

The window of time to witness a memorable event is can be fleeting, maybe lasting just a few seconds. My 5-year old son and I briefly witnessed something strangely unforgettable. He came to work with me before I had to drop him off for his afternoon kindergarten class.

Dan liked coming to work so he could eat sugar cubes by our coffee maker. Coloring books and puzzles usually kept him busy during these visits. This time I thought he might enjoy seeing how we made our own silicone rubber membrane, a critical component of our artificial lung. It was made using a dough mixer and another machine that poured a thin liquid silicone rubber coating over a plastic mesh that sat atop a continuous two-foot-wide roll of aluminum foil. The silicone rubber coating over the mesh on top of this aluminum foil was heated (cured), while moving for about 10 seconds along a 20-foot conveyor belt. My young son would certainly marvel at the intricate machinery and moving parts.

We were all very excited to be able to produce our own silicone rubber membrane. Making it was only a recent breakthrough for SciMed. I knew my boss Art was making membrane that morning. When I asked my son if he would like to see something very interesting, he said yes and off we went.

Art was a chemist at heart. Along with his executive duties, SciMed gave him a chance to be a chemist again and he loved it. He was a warm and caring person who counselled me to not work as hard as he had. Art deeply regretted time lost as a father and husband. But he was extremely proud of having designed and assembled the equipment used to make thin, high quality silicone rubber membrane for our artificial lung.

He was obviously having problems during the ten seconds or so my son and I were there to see him making membrane. Normally, finished membrane came off the conveyor belt and was automatically wound onto a large take-up roll for storage. But today Art decided to hold the membrane on the aluminum foil in his outstretched arms. He was doing this so he could inspect it inch by inch as it came off the conveyor belt. Art had a very frenzied look when we arrived. He obviously forgot to consider how fast membrane came off the conveyor belt.

There he was, totally unsure about what to do. The aluminum foil and its membrane kept spilling from his outstretched arms onto the floor. Yards and yards of it lay crinkled, crumpled and folded everywhere on the floor. It was a huge mess growing rapidly by the second, until Art realized the need to shut the machinery down.

There is an old proverb "out of the mouth of babes..." comes truth and wisdom. My son must have been impressed by what he saw because he asked: "Daddy, is this a machine to crinkle aluminum foil?" What could I say? That was certainly one interesting interpretation of what we saw!

Not wanting embarrass Art any further, we left quickly.

# Oops

**What I Learned:** *Savoring the special times in your personal life means letting go of things bothering you in your professional life,*

"Preoccupied" could have been my middle name during most of my SciMed tenure. I started each day optimistic about what tasks on my "to do" list I could get done. But within an hour, some new, urgent problem usually arose that had to be addressed immediately. I rarely finished much in a timely, efficient manner. My initial optimism was quickly lost, as my planned activities morphed into "organized chaos."

At home, I was almost always preoccupied about some lingering problem at work. These thoughts robbed me of quality down time ... time to relax or enjoy life's good experiences. I distinctly remember that work problems whirled through my mind while listening to Thursday night Orchestra Hall concerts with my wife. I went there to enjoy the music I loved. But I was robbed of the opportunity to enjoy it. True quality time was a rarity.

A very memorable distraction occurred on a glorious Sunday summer afternoon. I took my three kids and our dog Duchess to Oak Hill Park in St. Louis Park. I was determined to wipe any thoughts of work from my mind and just enjoy having fun with my kids. On the way home, I was pleased that I did not let any work distraction ruin my afternoon with the kids.

In the midst of a very intense, intimate marital moment that night with my wife, I suddenly jumped up and screamed, "I left the dog in the park!"

Naturally, I immediately went to the park with a flashlight to find Duchess in the dark. She was my sister's dog and had come to live with us three years earlier. "Duchess ... Duchess," I called out to no avail. I searched the entire park that night looking for her with no luck.

The next morning, I told my kids, "Daddy did a very bad thing." They starting crying, after I told them what happened. To calm them, I promised to look in the park again for Duchess. I had just enough time to do it before I had to leave to catch my plane for a trip out East.

I found Duchess immediately, waiting in the park's parking lot. If you think that dogs don't show emotion, you are wrong. Clearly, she looked "pissed."

When I look back at what happened, I wondered how I could have been so pre-occupied. Why did I suddenly think about our dog during such an intimate moment? What did that say about our marriage?

# I Should Have Told You

**What I Learned:** *Humor can be an effective communication tool. But consider if someone might misinterpret what you think is funny.*

I walked quickly through Denver's airport on a Friday afternoon with a broad smile on my face. I was smiling because this morning's open-heart surgery case went extremely well. It was a critical test of our artificial lung ... its first use at high altitude. Before this case, there was concern that our lung might not work as well at Denver's mile-high altitude where the oxygen content is lower.

I had just enough time to call Art and give him the good news before catching my flight home. "Everything worked great!" I told him. I ended our brief conversation, by telling him about a seemingly funny tidbit about the case: "The patient woke up hallucinating that he was in the Denver airport."

Art rushed into my office, as soon as I arrived at SciMed on Monday morning. I could tell that he was very disturbed about something.

"I can't find any reason why the Denver patient hallucinated," he exclaimed. "I've called surgeons using our lung, spoke with our vendors, checked with manufacturing and searched our records. I just don't know why this happened."

"We don't need to worry about anything," I responded. "The patient had mental problems before

46

his heart surgery. Having surgery helped his cardiac condition, but it was not going to cure any mental defect. I guess I should have told you about his mental condition when we talked on Friday."

# A Great VA Story

**What I Learned:** *Rules always make sense to those who make them. When there is a pressing need to bend one, prepare yourself for an avalanche of push-back and pain.*

D r. Charlie Helton was a great story teller. He was one of the highly motivated members of the University of Minnesota's Cardiac Surgical Research Team. His quiet nature and non-descript facial expression masked the real Charlie ... intelligent, witty and unafraid to pursue his convictions. Charlie also worked in the emergency department at the Minneapolis Veterans Administration (VA) Hospital as part of his University of Minnesota surgical residency training.

By this time, the team had already used our lung to breathe for a few patients. It always worked well. But no one survived because their underlying lung condition never healed. While at the VA Hospital, Charlie was always on the lookout for an acute lung failure patient who might be a good candidate for our artificial lung. If he found one, the University's team would willingly treat this patient using our lung.

He told me about rejecting one patient who was nearly dead. Once again, the staff waited far too long before asking Charlie if the patient was a good candidate. To make the point to refer patients sooner, he told the VA staff in jest that "rigor mortis" was a definite contraindication for artificial lung use.

I heard several other interesting Minneapolis VA Hospital stories. Some were about a unique arrangement a few VA surgeons had with some local morticians. These morticians would notify the surgeons if a deceased body had an implanted pacemaker. It was easy to know because the large size pacemakers created a very noticeable bulge in the overlying skin. One of these surgeons would go to the mortuary and pay a small fee to retrieve the implanted pacemaker. It, in turn, would be cleaned, sterilized and then implanted in another VA patient to save money. The best story though was about a patient in terrible pain that Charlie saw one Friday afternoon in the VA Hospital's emergency room.

Charlie determined that this patient's overwhelming pain was due to severe constipation. He asked his attending nurse to give the patient an enema. She told him that neither he nor any emergency room staff member could give an enema to a walk-in patient. It could only be given to a hospitalized patient.

But Charlie was determined to help this patient immediately. His surgical training had instilled the need without hesitation to pursue the best course of action, after quickly weighing all the risks of doing or not doing it. Once the nurse left, he gave the enema himself. It brought instant pain relief to the patient.

It did not take long for the emergency department supervisor to learn what happened. She admonished Charlie. He was told again that an enema could only be given to patients who were admitted into the hospital for treatment. Walk-in patients could not get treatment. To his dismay, it did not matter how impractical the policy was. Nor did it matter that the enema worked and saved the hospital a lot of money. This patient should have been hospitalized beforehand!

Charlie shrugged off this rebuke as just another example of bureaucratic craziness. He left the hospital a few hours later. Unbeknownst to Charlie, the emergency department supervisor chased after the discharged patient. She found him at the hospital's bus stop and convinced him to check into the Hospital that Friday afternoon.

When Charlie returned at Noon on Saturday, he was told to see his hospitalized patient. Charlie was confused by this directive, since he was not treating any hospitalized patients. To his surprise, it was the same patient he had given an enema to the day before. Finding absolutely nothing wrong with him, Charlie tried to discharge this patient … but he could not. VA Hospital policy then was that Saturday Noon was the latest time a patient could be discharged over the weekend. Charlie was able to discharge the patient Monday morning.

"That patient had a $600 enema," he said. Today that enema would have cost several thousand dollars.

# Breath of Life

***What I Learned:*** *A lot of unexpected things happen at work. Savor the good ones, since most are not!*

My day began with an unexpected telephone call from Jeff Howe. Jeff was the heart-lung technician on the University of Minnesota's Cardiac Surgical Research Team. He and I were close colleagues, having spent many hours working to ready SciMed's artificial lung for use in open-heart surgery.[3] Jeff was a tall, good looking guy whose regular work-outs gave him a great physique. A true "Renaissance" man, his personal interests and pursuits varied widely. His homespun sense of humor and philosophy made for enjoyable conversations. He said "Nick (Dr. Demetre Nicoloff) wants you to attend our last animal case today. It is the last one before we start using your lung in some open-heart surgery procedures."

There was never enough time to get everything done. When Jeff called, I had to quickly decide if I should accept this invitation. I did not foresee any reason why Nick wanted me to come, but I assumed there must be some good reason I was invited. So I accepted and off I went to the university. A few hours away from the office might be a refreshing change of pace.

Nick was a great guy ... smart, generous and warm-hearted. I knew him, since we took some graduate

---

3   Helton CW, Johnson FW, Howe JB, Freedman FB. Lindsay WG and Nicoloff DM. Development of a practical membrane lung system. Annals of Thoracic Surgery, July 1978; volume 28 (1): 54-61.

classes together. By now, his cardiac surgical research team had used our artificial lung on seven or eight acute lung failure patients. Our lung worked well, but none of them could be weaned off the heart-lung machine keeping them alive. Still it gave Nick ample confidence to start using our lung for certain open-heart surgery cases. I knew about this decision but did not know what type of cases he had in mind.

Baboons were used in cardiovascular research, since their cardiovascular anatomy and physiology are very similar to humans. When I arrived at the animal laboratory, one had already been anesthetized and was connected to the heart-lung machine. Our lung's shiny white outer cover made it very visible among the multitude of equipment and tubing being used. The baboon was peacefully asleep, unaware that he was undergoing a challenging open-heart surgery procedure.

Toward the end of the case, Nick told me that this baboon research allowed his team to gain enough experience to use our artificial lung in upcoming heart-lung transplant cases. That was exciting news! With a smile on his face, he then told me that this baboon was named "Frank" after me. I knew that research baboons were named after team members or close colleagues. Having one named after me was a distinct honor; it meant I was considered to be part of the team. I alone treasured this honor.

None of my colleagues, friends or family members understood why I felt so honored to have had a baboon named after me

It normally would have taken a few hours after "Frank's" case was finished for him to wake up from anesthesia, attend to his recovery and clean everything up. But it only took an hour because of an urgent call for help from the university's respiratory care unit.

A young motorcycle accident victim named Roger was dying, in spite of mechanical ventilation and other therapies. His lungs had filled with body fluid due to trauma suffered in the accident. He was literally drowning in his own body fluids. We went to the respiratory care unit. I might not be returning to work anytime soon, if Roger would be placed on a heart-lung machine using our lung to breathe for him.

Next to Roger in the respiratory care unit lay Karl Kassulke. Karl was a local Viking football team hero who in a split second became a quadriplegic due to a tackle gone bad. In the last few weeks, his breathing had become increasingly difficult. He was not able to breathe on his own. On Roger's other side lay the nine-month pregnant wife of a well-known Medtronic executive I knew from local professional meetings. Her life had also changed in an instant when she was rear-ended at high speed while waiting for a traffic light to turn green. Now she was lying paralyzed in the respiratory care unit, fighting just to breathe and stay alive.

Dr. Nicoloff was compassionate yet deliberate while talking with Roger's mother. He explained that our artificial lung could be used to keep Roger alive. Hopefully it would be long enough for the fluid in his lungs to clear. For some reason, she sought consolation and advice from me. Should the artificial lung be used to breath for her son? I had mixed feelings about giving any response. It was a chance to see another acute lung failure case at the university. But would I be crossing an ethical line by saying anything? I decided to give her the best counsel I could, as both a bioengineer and a father. Her son was dying in spite of receiving the best care possible. In retrospect, I should have at least told her that it was my company's artificial lung that might be used. Being ethical would have demanded this disclosure.

Roger was put on the bedside heart-lung machine, using our artificial lung. Jeff spent most of the next few days at Roger's bedside, making sure the heart-lung machine was working properly. Occasionally another heart-lung technician would relieve him for a few hours. The surgical residents from the team and Nick took turns stopping by to make any necessary adjustments to Roger's care and the heart-lung machine's operation. I spent many hours keeping Jeff company, giving him mostly emotional support while enjoying our camaraderie. I was hoping Roger would be our first University of Minnesota survivor.

While our lung worked well and Roger's condition was stable, he was still unable to breathe on his own as the third day began. To make matters worse, he needed many, many units of blood to offset blood lost by internal bleeding. Bleeding was expected, since anti-coagulants were given to patients on a heart-lung machine to prevent internal blood clotting, which could be fatal.

After consulting with the attending physician, Nick got approval to lavage Roger's lungs. Lavage would involve inserting a hollow plastic tube into Roger's lungs and applying suction to draw fluid from deep inside his airways. Since our artificial lung was breathing for him, very aggressive suction could be used to draw fluid out of his lungs. It worked. Within a few minutes, Roger started to breathe comfortably on his own. He now needed only minimal aid from his mechanical ventilator and was able to be discharged a few days later.

It took a while to sink in. I had witnessed the first successful acute lung failure case at the university. Someone was saved! I was so very thankful to have witnessed his survival. It was a definite roller coaster "high" ... almost a miracle! I think about Roger from time to time and wonder how is he doing

I attended all acute respiratory failure cases lung at the university. Typically, I was there continuously for almost a full day or more. I was exhausted from attending most of Roger's case. No wonder I was pulled over mid-day by the St. Louis Park Police on my way home.

"Are you drunk?" the officer asked. "Your car was weaving a lot."

"No sir," I replied. "I've been up for almost 48 hours helping with a case at the university. I'm exhausted." And so thankfully he escorted me safely home, just a few miles away.

I later learned that Karl survived and was released from the hospital. He went on to live a relatively long life. I'm not sure what happened to the other patient. This story's title "Breath of Life" was taken from the title of several U.S. newspaper stories about how our lung saved a patient.

# I Screwed Up

**What I Learned:** *If I screwed up or created a problem, it's always best that you first hear about it from me.*

Like a freight train gathering speed as it begins its journey, the company's achievements were coming at a faster pace as it journeyed through its fourth year. Eight U.S. hospitals were now using our artificial lungs for many of their open-heart surgery cases. We were also selling several dozen artificial lungs worldwide each month to treat acute lung failure. A tiny version of our artificial lung was being used for premature babies with hyaline membrane disease. These tiny babies responded well to this life-saving support.

SciMed finally hired its first salesman, which gave me more time to work on assigned technical projects at the company's facility. One of my first responsibilities was to develop a reliable in-house source of ultra-pure water. Purified water was used throughout the artificial lung manufacturing process. I was proud of the water treatment system I developed. It worked extremely well and required very little routine maintenance.

Since it was proving to be a trouble-free way to make ultra-pure water, I stopped paying much attention to the system after a few months. That gave me still more time to tackle a long list of important unfinished projects. Ignoring the water treatment system was a big mistake!

This mistake became apparent when one set of independent tests indicated a water quality problem.

Consequently, I had to tell a lot of people that a month's total output of packaged, sterilized artificial lungs residing in quarantine and finished goods could not be shipped. In terms of today's dollars, that amounted to over 50 thousand dollars' worth of product that was unusable due to my lack of sufficient oversight. To add to our woes, the affected products had to be disassembled and reworked to correct this problem. No new lungs could be manufactured for almost two weeks until I determined what went wrong and how to fix it.

Everyone knew I screwed up and my excuse for doing so, since I told them. Still, a lot of employees kidded me about my screw-up. The kidding was starting to get to me. After a few days, I realized it was not going to stop soon even though I had freely admitted my mistake. I had to acknowledge in a way that would stop the kidding and teasing. I thought of a way that might work!

The next day I snuck into our large clean room where the lungs were assembled. I went there when everyone was on coffee break. I brought my youngest child's record player and *Sesame Street* record with me. One of the songs on the record was perfect for what I wanted to do. I quickly put on the special clean room clothing. No one walking by the Clean Room windows could see me. I grabbed the telephone there and accessed the company's public address (PA) system.

I played the song entitled "Everyone Makes Mistakes and So Do You." It was a lively upbeat song about admitting to mistakes. Everyone in the building could hear it over our PA system.

I quickly shed my clean room clothing and raced through the building to see the response. Some people were singing the song. Others were clapping their hands or dancing to it. But our president was pissed. He ran through the building shouting, "Who did this? Where is it coming from? Turn it off!" I told him I did not know, when I passed him running back to get my daughter's phonograph and record.

Everyone in the building knew the culprit except him. No one ever said anything to the president. Of greater importance to me, the kidding stopped.

# Before There Was GPS

**What I Learned:** *Any decision is only as good as the validity of all underlying assumptions.*

I looked forward to returning to Boston. It was a great city to visit. I was there to meet with a prominent pediatric cardiac surgeon who was a close colleague of Dr. Nicoloff. Based on Nick's recommendation, he was interested in using our artificial lung in his complex pediatric open-heart cases. If he started using it, that would make him the second well-known pediatric cardiac surgeon using it.

I stayed at a motel that was just a few miles away from the hospital where our meeting would take place. Having been to Boston before, I felt comfortable renting a car to get around the city. I assumed that the rental car company map would suffice to guide me to the few hospitals I was going to visit.

I left early enough the next morning for my appointment with the pediatric cardiac surgeon. The map proved to be useless. It did not show enough key streets and buildings of interest. Guesses I made about where the hospital was located were all wrong. Boston's terrible drivers compounded my problem. They made it difficult to spend any time looking at my map. Cars on my right, for example, would suddenly pass and then cut in front of me to make a left turn into the next cross street. There was no place to park to spend time to scrutinize the map to find where I should be going. I became utterly lost and started to panic. I just couldn't miss this important meeting. It was the only time this surgeon could see me while I was in Boston.

Knowing precious time was slipping away, I did what I needed to do. I rented a taxi and followed it in my rental car to the hospital. I arrived just in time for my meeting. Naturally, it was hard to explain having both rental car and taxi expense receipts on my trip expense report.

Did I learn a lesson about driving in Boston? Yes, I did. I used a taxi for transportation around the city during my two subsequent visits there.

# Colored Tags

**What I Learned:** *Hindsight is rarely seen beforehand.*

At a staff meeting, I casually mentioned the importance of maintaining the quality of manufactured lungs. The president responded by asking me to establish and operate SciMed's first quality control unit. Lacking any training or experience, I just did what I thought were the right things to do. A young artistic woman was assigned to assist me. Like me, she was eager to work on this project. She too lacked any quality control training or experience.

One of my first assumed responsibilities was to temporarily quarantine each lot of newly packaged, sterilized products. These products had to stay in the quarantine room until they passed several quality tests. Since each test took a different amount of time to complete, I needed a way to distinguish one lot of artificial lungs from another. While temporarily stored in quarantine, I recorded which tests had been successfully completed for each lot of artificial lungs.

My artistic assistant suggested using different colored tags to distinguish one lot from another. Doing so would allow me to exactly indicate which products had passed what tests. I could tell anyone that, for example, "Products with blue tags could be released from quarantine." From there, they went to our finished goods inventory to fill orders. That approach seemed simple and reasonable to execute. It was adopted, making the quarantine room very colorful.

When all testing was successfully completed for any lot, I would page our teenage shipping clerk. He was a mellow young man who took delight in everything he did. I would tell him to what colored-tag products could be released from quarantine. I'd say something like, "Take the lot products with green tags to finished goods," which he did. I was proud of how easy it was to use colored tags to identify the different lots of quarantined products

About five years later, I was invited back as a guest to the visit the now successful company. I was given a tour. My tour guide was the same teenage shipping clerk, now a young man. When I saw the quarantine room, I asked him where the colored tags were? Aren't they being used?

"Oh no" he replied. "We stopped using them when your replacement found out that I was color blind."

"How did you know what products to take from quarantine?" I asked.

"I always had to ask someone else to point out which products had the colored tags you were talking about," he responded. "Then I knew which ones to take to finished goods."

My seemingly simple approach of using colored tags years ago did not consider colorblindness. I should have known better, but I didn't.

# Saturday Mornings

*What I Learned:* Being preoccupied can be an occupational hazard that blurs the line between your professional world and your personal life.

'd been with the company for almost six years. For the last few years, I always looked forward to playing tennis on Saturday mornings with my friend Louie, an easy-going guy with a warm smile and a great sense of humor. He always had a few interesting stories to tell. I started wondering why he almost always beat me in our first set of tennis, while I usually beat him in our second set. When I finally figured it out, I told him what I concluded the next time we played.

"Louie, you've been a big help to me on Saturday mornings." He looked puzzled as I continued.

"During the first set we play, I am always thinking about something at work I was angry or frustrated about. By the second set, I am no longer distracted by anything about work. That's why I usually beat you in the second set. Without you knowing it, you've been my Saturday morning psychiatrist."

Louie's puzzled look turned to a big smile as he asked, "So how much can I bill you for these visits?"

# "What the Hell Is Going On?"

**What I Learned:** *Knowing when to keep your mouth shut is important. Some may count it as a blessing.*

I vividly remembered my last trip to Boston and my need to use a taxi to get around. About six months later, I returned to train a team of heart-lung technicians how to use our artificial lung. Training would be done during an actual open-heart surgery case when a mechanical heart valve would be implanted.

The technicians were easy to train. The heart-lung machine, with our artificial lung, was quickly set up and ready for use. The patient was anesthetized and connected to the heart-lung machine. Surgery began. It took the Surgeon just a few minutes to crack open the chest, cut through the heart wall and removed the diseased heart valve. He then determined what size replacement mechanical heart valve would fit correctly in the opening created by removing the diseased valve.

The circulating nurse was told to get that size valve from their inventory. Everything was going well. The technicians seemed pleased. Our lung was working perfectly. This case was off to a good start and seemed relatively simple, compared to the complex open-heart surgery cases I usually attended.

Moments later the nurse returned. You could see a sense of panic in her face. With great hesitation she announced, "We don't have that size valve in stock."

The surgeon was a tall imposing man who could easily command attention with just a quiet word or simple look. But he was clearly angry as he shouted, "What the hell is going on? Why don't we have one? How many times have I told you to check that we have everything needed before each case. God damn it. How many times have I asked you to make a checklist?" That was the last coherent ranting I remember before he unleashed his full anger in a torrent of sharp, hurtful four-letter expletives.

It took a little over an hour to locate the right size heart valve at another local hospital and transport it to the waiting surgeon and his surgical team. Meanwhile, the patient remained on the heart-lung machine. While prolonged time on a heart-lung machine with a conventional artificial lung can damage blood elements and make recovery problematic, the surgeon knew that use of our lung greatly reduced this risk. His mood gradually changed from anger to acceptance during this hour.

He tried to make light of this delay, but the tension in that operating room was palpable. His attempts at casual conversation and a few jokes were barely acknowledged by the surgical team he had just humiliated. I knew he was embarrassed that a visitor was witnessing this major screw-up.

I wanted to say something, anything to ease the tension in the room. One side of my brain told me to say nothing. Don't risk alienating the surgeon. The other side told me to "Go for it ... say something funny to ease the tension in the room." This time I said nothing. I kept my big mouth shut.

The surgeon completed the procedure without incident in a little less time than it took to get the heart valve. Our product worked well throughout the case. The surgery was successful and recovery was smooth and uneventful. It was a good example of a case lasting much longer than anticipated, with our artificial lung making it safe for the patient to be on the heart-lung machine for several hours. If a conventional artificial lung would have been used, this patient's recovery could have been problematic.

I found it humorous how the heart valve got to the hospital. It was not brought there by a police cruiser, medical van, ambulance or even a hospital panel truck. It came to the hospital by a taxi.

The surgeon asking for a "checklist" several times made me think. It seemed like a very logical idea to have one. But I could not ever recall one being used in any open-heart surgery case I attended for SciMed.

Ironically, I sat next to a commercial airline pilot on my flight home from this trip. I asked him how important a check list was. His responded by saying, "I never assumed that the flaps are up and the wheels are down when landing, unless my copilot read it back to me as 'done' from our check list."

What I had witnessed was a valuable example of how a seemingly short, simple open-heart surgery case can unexpectedly be prolonged. Use of our lung during the prolonged operation contributed to an uneventful patient recovery.

I should have enjoyed this trip more than I did. It was certainly successful, and it took place in one of my favorite cities. But unknowingly it was the next to last time I attended an open-heart surgery before SciMed's president fired me.

# Toward Profitability

**What I Learned:** *Being creative served me better than all my college courses and formal training.*

Open-heart surgeons were always concerned about the safety of patients who had to remain on a heart-lung machine much longer than anticipated. Heart surgeons knew that conventional artificial lungs used in heart-lung machines during the 1970's damaged blood elements if used for much more than an hour or so. This damage caused serious problems for recovering patients. While academic and research-savvy surgeons began using our artificial lung in the longer or more complex open-heart cases, surgeons practicing in the community setting were reluctant to do so. Their experience told them that only a few cases ever lasted much longer than an hour. Therefore, they could not justify asking their hospital administrators to spend about a hundred dollars more to use an artificial membrane lung like ours.

I had to figure out how surgeons could justify the extra hundred-dollar cost to use our lung on every case. They did not buy the argument than an extra hundred dollars added very little to cases costing thousands of dollars in supplies and medications. It did not matter that surgeons using them for pediatric and complex adult open-heart surgery cases were very pleased with them.

If SciMed was to become profitable, we had to convince more cardiac surgeons that the added cost to use our artificial lung was justifiable for their routine cases. A creative flash sparked an idea that worked.

I took a page from the insurance industry, adopting the script agents use to sell life insurance to young couples with children. First, they got prospective clients to talk about how much they cared about their close ones. Sometime prospective clients would say that they did not think they needed much insurance because they were young and healthy. Whether or not they said that, the agent would ask them if they knew anyone in their 30s or 40s who died due to an accident, sudden onset of aggressive cancer, etc. A good insurance policy would be sold, if it was viewed as a way to limit a major potential financial risk.

I used the same approach to get surgeons to use our artificial lung for their open-heart surgery cases ... reducing the potential risks of postoperative complications and the costs to treat them. First, I would get surgeons to indicate that they really cared a lot about their patients. Then, I would guide them to acknowledge that risks unexpectedly arise occasionally when a routine case goes afoul. From there, I posed five questions to get them thinking more positively about routine use of our lung in their cases:

"Do you occasionally have cases that unexpectedly take much more than an hour to complete?" The answer was usually "yes."

"In such cases, do you worry that those patients might experience serious, costly complications during recovery?" The answer was usually "yes."

"Are you aware that the SciMed artificial lung is relatively safe to use for extended period of time?" The answer was usually "yes."

"Would you feel more comfortable using the SciMed artificial lung, if you knew ahead of time that a case might take up to six hours to complete?" The answer was usually "yes."

"Do you generally know ahead of time which cases might unexpectedly take up to six hours to complete?" The answer was usually "no."

This line of questioning helped surgeons realize the trade-offs between using or not using our artificial lung. Routine use might definitely benefit a relatively small percentage of their patients. But it was impossible to know which ones might benefit before each case began. If our lung was used for all patients, the ones who needed it would experience fewer post-operative complications and shorter hospital stays. Surgeons knew that difficult patient recoveries due to prolonged use of current artificial lungs were very costly, far exceeding ten thousand dollars. By asking them to add up the cost of using our lung for all their cases, many were able to conclude that the hundred-dollar extra cost to use our lung for every patient was far less than the cost of just a few difficult patient recoveries. Routine use of our artificial lung started to seem justifiable.

This approach gained some success when I talked to surgeons about using our lung. Our small sales staff adopted this approach, generating substantially more product sales. SciMed would soon be profitable.

# A Memorable Open-Heart Surgery Case

***What I Learned:*** *Some days when your curtain goes up, the script written for you will create a lifetime memory.*

During my last year at SciMed, I ran the quality control department and helped fixed problems that arose in production. A few times I helped with minor problems that surgeons had using our lung. I no longer attended open-heart surgery cases, since our small sales force had assumed this responsibility.

When SciMed hired our third president, it was making progress on all fronts. He was outwardly a quiet, impeccably dressed man who had just retired from an executive position at another company. SciMed was then well along the path of becoming profitable in less than a year. However, it was my impression that he took this job just to coast through his last year of work until he retired for good.

In my role as SciMed's de-facto troubleshooter, I was often the person telling our President about potential and ongoing problems and my plans to address them. He really disliked hearing about problems and, by association, disliked me. His facial expressions and manner when talking to me reluctantly led me to this conclusion. In my mind, he was just tolerating my presence until others could assume my responsibilities and make me very dispensable. And I sensed that time was coming soon.

I was not expecting to attend another open-heart surgery procedure. Nor was I expecting to be fired either. Events leading up to both occurrences played out on a stage that had been set much earlier.

One day, some of us learned that several open-heart patients had died quite unexpectedly at one hospital, either during their surgery or shortly thereafter. Our artificial lung did not work properly in these cases. We were told little else. It was extremely upsetting news. Death during open-heart surgery was a known, but rare occurrence. But death of several patients within a short time span at one hospital was unheard of … a sign of a major problem!

A meeting was quickly convened to review these deaths and consider if they were due to our artificial lung. We knew that one key component used to manufacture it was recently changed. It was disturbing to learn that the new component was less likely to remain stabilized in a fixed position than the one previously used. If this component moved much during a surgical procedure, the artificial lung could fail to work properly.

I was relieved to hear that the new component would be stable, if heart-lung technicians were following our new instructions to set up the artificial lung for use. But when this contention was questioned, I was not sure if it had been thoroughly evaluated. That was troubling … but not troubling enough!

Toward the end of the meeting, the critical question on everyone's mind was about the few hospitals using artificial lungs made with the new component. Were they also using the new way to set up the artificial lung for surgery? My best guess was that they probably were not, since technicians hated making changes. And I was sure they were not told how important it was to use the new set-up. Therefore, I was asked to attend an open-heart surgery case where a lung made with the new component would be used. I was to make sure that the new instructions were followed.

I call some technicians I knew well who were using our lung at one Twin City hospital. They agreed to use the lung I would bring and follow the new operating instructions for the next day's first surgery case. To them, I was a trusted source of technical advice.

Next day in the operating room, the technicians followed the new instructions to set up the lung for use in the heart-lung machine. They even commented that the new way made it easier to set up the lung. About a half hour into the case. I could clearly see that the new component inside the lung was shifting and becoming distorted. The lung was showing early signs of failure. If the component shifted much more, it could produce a catastrophic failure! I briefly pondered some scary questions: "Would the failure progress?" "Would the patient die?" I should not have asked the technicians to use this lung!

I immediately alerted everyone in the operating room about the lung. The surgeon's brilliant thinking and the technicians' quick response allowed the case to continue without any adverse outcome. Like others in that operating room, I was terribly shaken by what I saw. I concluded that failure could occur, regardless of whether or not the new instructions were followed. Only through the grace of God or some higher power was a catastrophe adverted.

I was asked to update our president, a few days later after I had finished thoroughly evaluating this problem. While my news was reasonably good, it would be one more time when I would have to tell him about some problem. And I would be discussing the most serious type of problem a medical device company could face. As I entered his office I thought about the old saying, "Don't shoot the messenger!"

A small smile quickly turned into a frown as he looked up from his desk and realized who was his office. He did not like hearing about the patient deaths and product failures again … even though I told him that simply reverting back to how our artificial lungs were previously made would solve the problem. There was other "good" news. We had acted quickly and responsibly to prevent further loss of life. The deaths had occurred at only one hospital. I sensed his growing anger. As I tried in vain to assure him that products made before the component change were safe to use, he suddenly fired me!

Being abruptly fired was devastating. It was like unexpectedly losing a child I helped bring into this world. SciMed was a huge part of my life. I loved my work there and pursued it with great passion and personal sacrifice.

Perhaps I was stupid or naïve, but I never thought about challenging my firing. I could have asked my fellow co-founders to back me. I could have asked our Board of Directors to reverse this decision. After all, I was a SciMed co-founder. Our third president was merely an outsider brought in to run the company. And he was not doing much to run it.

Even though I saw it coming, being fired was very hurtful. It was hard to understand, since I was fired right after I helped SciMed avert a company-ending crisis. These hurtful feelings came and went over the next year or so. But I never let them hinder my desire to "get back into the race." I got another job, a good one at Medtronic, five weeks after leaving SciMed.

It was also hurtful that none of my colleagues reached out to me after I was fired. They all knew there was no good reason why I was fired. I thought we were close colleagues, but evidently not friends.

During the rest of my long, rewarding career in the medical device industry, I occasionally recalled this last case and events associated with it. To this day, I am still haunted because some patients needlessly died, I lost the valued trust of a few technicians and my lack of foresight almost caused another death.

I went through hell writing this particular story. It was an incredibly painful, dark period in my life. I had horrible dreams and hardly slept at night on the days I took time to relive these events in sufficient detail to write this story.

# AFTERWORD

In retrospect, the deaths of several patients at the one hospital should not have happened. The safety of a product change deemed appropriately evaluated, in hindsight, was not. Ironically, my first major assignment at my next employer involved failures of another type of medical device ... pacemakers. Subsequent implementation of the U.S. Food and Drug Administration's medical device regulations made companies demonstrate the safety of new or changed products before they could be sold. Safety problems can still arise. When they do, the vast majority are properly addressed. Occasionally one is not, because an executive ignores it too long or fails to grasp how much harm it could cause.

I was surprised that none of my colleagues called or wrote me a note about my being fired.

My former Quality Assistant called me shortly after I left SciMed. She was fired without knowing why. When she said she had called her new boss a "jerk," I responded. "That's what got you fired."

A few years after I was fired, I reluctantly sold my SciMed stock to add a porch onto our house. The hundreds of thousands of dollars I expected to get from my $10,000 investment never materialized. But I gained satisfaction knowing that my work and our products had saved hundreds of patients with acute lung failure. It also made post-operative recovery safer and more comfortable for thousands of open-heart surgery patients. Our lung set the standard for the design of modern day artificial lungs.

I believe that my successes at SciMed fulfilled my mother's wish to "leave this earth in a little better shape than I found it." But that realization came only years later, after the pain of my dismissal lessened.

About five years after I left SciMed, an investor group bought our successful company and rewrote its history. They largely downplayed its role in advancing cardiac surgery patient support and care, while financing the effective transition to a still more profitable company. It concentrated its efforts developing and selling lucrative balloon angioplasty catheters. Its subsequent success led to it being purchased and becoming a highly-valued division of the Boston Scientific Corporation.

Our second president seemed to work harder at filling his social calendar than his job. But still I thought he helped SciMed progress. Since I thought we had a good relationship, I was pleased with his willingness to serve as a reference for jobs I sought after being fired. Sadly, I learned he gave very negative recommendations about me. I got the very next job I sought, using an alternate reference.

About seven years after I left SciMed we both were having lunch at the same restaurant, a few tables away from each other. We exchanged greetings. But I did not answer his question: "What are you working on these days?" I nodded my head back and forth and put a finger across my closed lips to indicate I wasn't going to respond. He asked again, now raising his voice a little. Again, I did not respond.

Still, he insisted on getting an answer. He repeatedly asked the same question, getting loud enough to gain the attention of more nearby diners. They were now listening to his repeated question and watching me try to indicate that I was not going to tell him what I did. But I finally stood up and loudly replied "ERECTILE DYSFUNCTION." That ended the questioning.

# Part Two
# MEDTRONIC INC.
# 1976 - 1983

Part Two describes my experience at Medtronic, a well-established pacemaker corporation during this period. I came to Medtronic as a "diamond in the rough." While I was successful at SciMed, I never knew why some things worked and others did not. Therefore, I looked forward to polishing my professional skills as a Medtronic employee.

I found it ironic that my termination from SciMed involved a major, hazardous product problem and my first substantial project at Medtronic also involved a major, hazardous product problem.

During my tenure there, I achieved many notable accomplishments and made a few substantial mistakes. While I received helpful formal training in retrospect perseverance, common sense and creativity proved far more valuable professionally than any training I received

I envisioned working at Medtronic for the rest of my career, not an unreasonable expectation then for a 36-year old professional like me. It took only a few months to realize that I had left one roller coaster ride at SciMed, only to begin another one at Medtronic. This time the highs and lows were more noticeable and frequent. The ride ended when a new boss terminated me a year or so after receiving a widely-distributed critical memo I wrote about him.

In my last year, I coined two phrases describing what I personally experienced: "Corporate Russian Roulette" and "Corporate Purgatory." Unfortunately, these phrases are still appropriate descriptors of what a multitude of corporate employees can experience in their careers.

# Here's What
# I'd Do

***What I Learned:*** *Humor in small doses can be used to apologize, change thinking or draw attention to something.*

During the afternoon of my first day of work, Medtronic announced the recall of a few lots of Xytron pacemakers in consultation with the U.S. Food and Drug Administration (FDA). Ultimately, every lot of Xytron pacemakers was recalled due to premature failures and Xytron production stopped.

One of my regulatory affairs departmental responsibilities was to provide regulatory support of Xytron pacemakers. All returned and inventoried Xytron pacemakers were destroyed, except for one lot that somehow languished in finished goods inventory. The manufacturing engineer responsible for them called me about extending their shelf-life. He did not realize that they should have been destroyed. Either he never got the memo about Xytron pacemakers or he just ignored it.

"What should I do with them?" he asked. He was puzzled by my response, "Just hire a contract-arsonist to steal them from inventory and burn them." That made him realize the need to destroy them.

The Corporation struggled with the enormity of these recalls, involving tens of thousands of pacemakers. It had to deal with patients who had a defective pacemaker, placate implanting physicians, figure out how to replace the recalled pacemakers, keep competitors from stealing their customers and respond to negative comments from stockholders and harsh directives from the FDA.

Most employees were very sympathetic about the fate of affected patients. Almost all patients were 70 years or older. They would be exposed to risks and discomfort of having their pacemaker removed and replaced by a new one. I did not foresee how our marketing organization would view this situation. They saw the recalls as an opportunity to increase sales ... a new pacemaker model had to be purchased to replace any one removed from a patient. That boosted sales, substantially. How's that for forward-thinking entrepreneurship?

Unexpectedly, Medtronic gained unwanted and embarrassing international notoriety from these recalls. This negative notoriety was due to how "Xytron" sounded when it was pronounced. It sounded very similar to the name of the poison gas the Nazis used in their gas chambers. Our European employees were probably never consulted about this brand name when it was proposed. If they were, it was 1976 and they were most likely too young to know much about this atrocious history.

Chuck Swanson, a regulatory affairs colleague at the time, thought I had some mystic insight about the Xytron recalls. He remembered me asking him on my first morning of work at Medtronic, if anything eventful was happening that I should know about. I merely asked this question to keep a casual conversation going with someone I just met. That afternoon, Medtronic unexpectedly announced its first Xytron recall. Chuck became a long-term consulting client many years later.

During those years and even recently, he expressed amazement that I had the insight to ask this question. I could never convince him otherwise.

# No Thanks Needed

**What I Learned:** *Sometimes a seemingly simple request turns into a very complex project.*

B esides providing regulatory support for certain Xytron and other Medtronic products, I also had to learn about Medtronic's documentation system. That is why I was asked to obtain all design, testing and manufacturing documents relating to five specific Xytron® pacemakers. They were part of the FDA recall of pacemakers whose batteries prematurely failed due to an electronic circuitry problem. A legal defense team wanted these documents to help defend six company executives against criminal charges about these failures filed by the U.S. Department of Justice.

Medtronic's documentation system was a mystery to almost everyone in the corporation. I assumed the responsibility to learn about it, since no one else in my department was willing to deal with this dreaded system. I learned a lot about the documentation system, once I accepted the fact that the rationale for how it was organized made no sense and it had some glaring shortcomings.

One shortcoming made it impossible to determine exactly which design, testing and manufacturing files applied to these five pacemakers. While only several dozen files were needed, there were dozens and dozens of files to choose from. That meant about 100,000 pages of documentation had to be reviewed to decide which files were most likely the correct ones to provide to the legal defense team.

I formed and led a company-wide team of volunteers to review the files and identify the most likely several dozen needed. With the strong support of my immediate boss, I led the team for four or five weeks. Team members willingly undertook this unplanned project, even though they still had to perform their regular job duties. To do so, they all worked 60-75 hours weekly. I remember how difficult it was for many of us to even take four hours off then to attend a family Thanksgiving Day dinner.

The corporate executive in charge of our department did not want anyone from regulatory affairs to work on this project, even though I was uniquely qualified to do so. He did not think it was our responsibility to obtain the files. He replaced me with an auditor, and admonished my boss for assigning me to lead this project.

I trained my replacement to recognize which documents were needed by the legal defense team. Then, I helped the legal defense team interpret and organize the hundreds of pages of documentation being provided to them. The executive fired my boss, once he learned I was still working on this project.

The files provided helped the legal defense team demonstrate that Medtronic followed "state-of-the-art" design, testing and manufacturing practices to produce these five Xytron pacemakers. In retrospect, state-of-the-art was no longer good enough for the newer technologies incorporated into these failed pacemakers. Since criminal intent was neither evident nor proven, all criminal charges were dropped.

Work on this project made me an expert about our documentation system and its shortcomings. After it was completed, I shared my expertise in a corporate-wide presentation. My replacement learned a lot from me and from working on this project. He went on to become the corporation's compliance expert, someone with the skills to know how to respond to requests from the FDA for information when there was ambiguity about what information to provide.[4]

I asked and then begged the executive to personally thank team members. They had worked almost double shifts for many weeks to obtain the files needed for this project. He strongly disagreed that any acknowledgement was due and said "NO." I was very angry that he saw no reason to thank them.

Many years later this executive was in another company and I was a practicing consultant. He left me several telephone messages about referring my consulting clients who needed his assistance to him. I delighted in never answering any of his requests for referrals.

---

[4]  Subsequently, the FDA enacted regulations. These regulations were intended to prevent documentation (and other types of medical device) shortcomings from occurring. By then, Medtronic had already remedied them.

# Don't
# Say Anything

***What I Learned:*** *Posing a question is sometimes a better way to communicate a request or suggestion than a statement telling someone to do something.*

New employees were given a chance to observe a pacemaker implant, as part of their corporate orientation training. I welcomed the chance to observe a pacemaker implant at Ramsey County Hospital (now Regions Hospital).

During orientation, we were told repeatedly to not say anything while we observed an implant in the operating room. From my SciMed operating room experience, I knew it was an appropriate directive. I faithfully followed it, until the hospital's electricity failed during the procedure I attended.

An emergency generator kicked in immediately. That restored some of the lost electrical power. But only a few lights were lite in the operating room. There was not enough light to allow the surgeon to clearly see the operating field. He kept asking the two attending nurses for more light to continue implanting the pacemaker. In response, the nurses took turns opening the operating room door and yelling into the hallway that the doctor needed more light to finish the case. Otherwise, they did nothing to help him see better.

I could see a large flashlight in a supply cabinet near me. Remembering the directive to not say anything, I was very reluctant to call attention to it. But it was hard to restrain myself. The surgeon kept asking for enough light to see better; the nurses' frantic calls for help into the hallway were not heeded. Completing the pacemaker implant was impossible.

I took a chance and pointed to the large flashlight in the operating room's supply cabinet, posing this question to the circulating nurse: "Do you think the doctor might want to use the flashlight in this cabinet to help him see better?"

She wasn't sure if he would want it ... but I was. After I gently asked again, she decided it was a good idea. The surgeon was thrilled to use the flashlight to illuminate the operating field. The pacemaker was successfully implanted without any negative consequences.

I never told anyone at work about this incident, since I had disobeyed the directive to say nothing.

# Bittersweet Successes

***What I Learned:*** *Failure can be snatched away from the jaws of success.*

D ave Juncker hired me to be project manager for the pacing leads development department. A pacing lead has insulated wires that electrically connect the pacemaker to the heart. One end of the lead is inserted into the pacemaker. Electrodes at the other end are placed inside the heart. The electrodes enable the pacemaker to sense the heart's electricity to determine if a heart-beat might be missed. If so, the pacemaker would deliver a tiny electrical stimulus to make the heart beat then and not skip a beat.

I enjoyed working for Dave. We had been close colleagues in graduate school (University of Minnesota) and later in Medtronic's regulatory affairs department. His strengths were a keen sense of humor, an ability to envision the "big picture" and a warm, inviting personality. His was an active mind that produced a never-ending list of ideas to consider. Conversations with Dave could wander from one topic to another. Dave was a caring and inspiring manager.

If you want exercise and notoriety, become a project manager at Medtronic. I walked many miles each day to meet with project team members, throughout the sprawling corporate complex. Fortunately, the notoriety I gained was all positive. The three major projects I managed while working for Dave all were successfully completed. But each success was bittersweet.

The first major project was to identify which type of pacemaker adapter storage kits should be made available to physicians. Implanting physicians had to use a pacemaker adapter to electrically connect a new Medtronic pacemaker to an already implanted competitor's pacing lead. That's because pacemaker and lead manufacturers used different types of electrical connectors. Collectively, physicians implanting Medtronic pacemakers would require a relatively large number of different pacemaker adapter models. The project involved determining which types of adapters should be packaged together in a kit. It also involved determining how many different types of kits should be made to meet the needs of all physicians for pacing adapters?

I formed a team with a packaging engineer and a design engineer to pursue this project. We determined that Medtronic would have to inventory a large number of different types of adapter kits to meet the vast array of physician needs. Doing so would create a substantial financial burden. The packaging engineer offered a great solution to this dilemma; he proposed to just provide an attractive, empty storage container with inserts to store the various types of adapters each physician needed. Labels would be also provided with the containers to indicate where the various adapter models were stored within the container. This approach would allow physicians to customize their storage container and store only the specific adapter models they needed. His idea saved Medtronic over $100,000 (circa late-1970s) of inventory costs. He left Medtronic for another job that did not last very long. When he tried to return to Medtronic, he was told that he was not qualified to assume his former packaging engineering job.

The second major project was adding a new, inex-pensive accessory inside the pacing lead packaging. Its use made it much easier for inexperienced physicians to insert a pacing lead into the bloodstream, so it could then be advanced toward the heart. Marketing hoped its availability might entice cardiologists who were reluc-tant to implant pacing leads to start implanting them. Since that could be expected to boost sales of pacing leads, marketing planned to heavily promote this new accessory and its immediate availability at an upcoming major medical conference.

This became a major project, since It had to be done so quickly. The schedule only allowed two months for packaging, regulatory, labeling and sterilization changes to be completed. Because this was a high-pri-ority, unplanned project, those working on it still had to perform their normal job duties. Never-the-less, all activities were successfully completed within two-months ... except for one.

Unfortunately, our Puerto Rico manufacturing facility delayed adding the new accessory into pack-aged pacing leads. They definitely got the new acces-sories, packaging and everything else needed to start in a timely manner. They also were told to make this change immediately. But they decided to save money by using up their current stock of packaging items first, not wanting to incur the financial cost of scrapping their existing packaging. The accessory would not even start being added in the pacing lead packages until weeks after the medical conference. Can you imagine how angry marketing was to learn about this delay?

The third major project involved developing a new family of pacing lead models that used polyurethane as the insulating material instead of silicone rubber. Pacing leads made with polyurethane insulation were much easier to implant than silicone rubber insulated leads. Patients would benefit from the smaller size of these leads. Developing them was an important, high visibility project.

Two polyurethane lead models were completely developed and tested under my direction before I left my job as a project manager. I decided to leave this position for a promotion to become the director of clinical research. My successor was very eager to take over. She took on this high-visibility project to gain recognition of her technical and leadership skills. Under her project leadership, development of additional polyurethane pacing lead models seemed to be going well after I left.

One unspoken rule I learned in engineering college was to "always leave a project on the way up." That rule proved invaluable for the polyurethane lead project. Short-term clinical research studies that Medtronic performed demonstrated that polyurethane-insulated leads were safe and worked well. But a small and growing number of anecdotal reports later indicated something different. Polyurethane leads implanted for longer periods were not safe due to insulation failures. They were ultimately the subject of several product recalls and lawsuits. The very capable colleague who took over for me unknowingly inherited a nightmare ... depositions, courtroom testimonies, patient deaths, etc.

# Please Don't Come Any More

***What I Learned:*** *Sometimes the job requires a man-*
*ager to be a coach. If you take*
*the time to do so, it can be a*
*labor of love.*

The clinical research department's role was to obtain the clinical experience required to support the needs of many other departments (design, marketing, regulatory affairs, etc.), before a new pacemaker or pacing lead could be sold. It was no secret that this department was in disarray, when I became its director. On my very first day as director, I was greeted with a continuing stream of telephone complaints, some angrily expressed using four-letter expletives.

The professional staff was constantly subjected to criticism from others at Medtronic about what type of clinical experience was needed and how to obtain it. Frankly, they were demoralized when I took over.

Critical changes were necessary. That was why I was hired. I quickly convened a staff meeting to listen to their concerns and begin the process of making substantial changes. But I honestly did not have any specific ideas about what changes were necessary. It was hard to know if I would need a protective suit of amour, a big box of Kleenex or both to get through this meeting.

One by one, the staff told me about problems they faced. To their surprise (and mine), after a moment's thought I announced that they would now lead their clinical research studies differently. Those in charge of clinical studies would operate as "clinical study managers." This was a totally foreign concept to them. It was not how the department previously operated. As clinical study managers, their job would be to seek consensus from product development team members about what clinical experience was needed, what physicians to use as investigators and how to conduct the study. But if consensus was not possible, the clinical study manager alone would make the final decisions. It may have been the first use of project management to lead clinical studies in the Twin Cities or the entire medical device industry.

They expressed great reluctance to accept their new role. I was pointedly told that my approach was not how things were done. I countered by reminding them how difficult their jobs currently were … constantly reacting to criticism and unreasonable requests. Managing clinical research studies, rather than reacting to circumstances, would make them far more productive and make their jobs easier.

I decided to use the pending Spectrax® Pacemaker Clinical Study as the vehicle to introduce the corporation to the new way clinical research would be conducted. Spectrax was a revolutionary new type of pacemaker, one that could improve patient outcomes and boost the corporation's bottom line. Its leader, Tim Lathrop, was now the Spectrax "clinical study manager." Tim was a smart, popular scientist who had an engaging smile and warm personality. I don't think he had led any project in his life. Meetings he convened about the Spectrax clinical study were always disasters.

I also told Tim that I expected him to get at least 95 percent of clinical data expected from the Spectrax clinical study. In the past, getting far less clinical data returned sufficed because very little was required to evaluate older pacemaker models. Getting 95 percent of the data returned to us was critical for two compelling reasons: New FDA regulations would require it before approving Spectrax sales in the U.S. Marketing was depending upon it to support a planned, aggressive Spectrax sales campaign.

Tim understood why I picked the Spectrax clinical study to proactively introduce these changes to the corporation. But he was very hesitant to assume his new responsibilities. A colleague and I became his coaching staff. We talked with Tim daily to make him comfortable about assuming them. Each day for about a week, Tim left Medtronic more and more confident that he could assume this new role as "clinical study manager."

Each morning he would return to work with uncertainty about his ability to do so. We stopped coaching him when he started seeing the bigger picture. The corporation could no longer tolerate clinical studies whose outcomes were marginally useful due to confusion about what clinical experience was needed and how to obtain it.

To completely allay his fears, I sent a memo to the Spectrax development team about Tim's new role as a clinical study manager and his new responsibilities. I informed them that I planned to accompany Tim at the next team meeting in case any questions arose. At the meeting, I started to explain his new role and responsibilities. To his credit, he took over explaining his new responsibilities and how the Spectrax clinical study would be conducted.

After the meeting, Tim's first words to me were: "Please don't come to any more of these meetings. If you do, that could detract from my authority." He might have expected me to be angry. Instead and with a big smile, I shook his hand and exclaimed, "Congratulations ... You are where I need you to be."

All subsequent meetings Tim convened about the Spectrax clinical study were very productive. He became an outstanding clinical study manager.

The Spectrax Clinical Research Study was one of the most successful, effective studies ever performed at Medtronic. It drew praises from all across the company. I was especially pleased that my expectations for data were met; more than 95 percent of expected data was obtained for this study. This study reset the bar for clinical research study excellence, primarily using a project management approach to pursue it. Tim's success using my new approach for conducting clinical studies was a real "high."

# Hold Them in Receiving

**What I Learned:** *Try not to create your own problems.*

It was not easy to be a good father to my 12-year-old son. He was living with me, after my soon-to-be ex-wife threw him out of her home. He was struggling with being an adolescent, much more than I knew. When he asked me to take him to Wisconsin to buy some fireworks for the upcoming July 4th holiday, I agreed to go there with him the following weekend. It was a chance to support him.

Fireworks sold in neighboring Wisconsin were much better than those we could buy in Minnesota. But Wisconsin law then forbid non-residents from taking fireworks from the stores selling them. They would have to be shipped to me.

That created a problem.

We lived in an apartment that had no vestibule entrance or a caretaker there during daytime hours. That meant that I had to send the fireworks to Medtronic. I was told that the fireworks would arrive in a week. I called our receiving department the following Tuesday morning. I needed to alert them about what was coming ... two cartons containing fireworks. Each carton would have several large, bright iridescent orange "EXPLOSIVES" warning stickers on it. My plan was to get them as soon as they arrived on the loading dock to avoid any criticism or possible reprimand.

I apologized about my need to send the cartons to Medtronic. "Just call me when they arrive. You won't miss spotting them. I will come immediately and put them in my car."

"You are too late," I was told. "We just got them and sent them to incoming inspection."

"Oh my God. I could be in big trouble" I thought, as I rushed to Incoming Inspection. "Why was I stupid enough to send fireworks to Medtronic? What was I thinking?"

At incoming inspection, I was told that the cartons had just been sent to our central mail room. Obviously, the bright orange EXPLOSIVES warning stickers were not seen. Frantically, I rushed to the mail room to retrieve them. Could I head off exposing my bad decision to any more employees?

I arrived just a little too late I was told. The cartons were already on the mail cart sent all over the corporation to deliver mail and packages. "They will be at your desk within the hour," I was told.

They were on my desk when I returned from the mail room, two large cartons with bright orange "EXPLOSIVES" warning stickers. Wasn't anyone concerned that something dangerous was present?

But nothing happened. I was never admonished. No one even made a negative comment about my poor judgment. Dozens of employees saw the "EXPLOSIVES" stickers. Yet no one said or did anything about these cartons. The security guard politely said "hi" and held the front door open for me when I took them to my car. The old saying "asleep at the wheel" certainly applied to everyone who saw both cartons that day.

# The Little Boy Who Didn't Die

*What I Learned:* Always do the right thing.

Early during the Spectrax Pacemaker clinical study, we learned about a potentially serious problem with one little boy's implant. His parents were given a home monitoring telephone transmission instrument. They used it to faithfully send weekly telephone transmissions to Medtronic and the Mayo Clinic where this pacemaker was implanted. The transmissions would allow us to know how well the pacemaker was working. This was especially important, since this little boy was a rare pacemaker-dependent patient. That meant his tiny heart needed almost constant pacing to keep beating continuously.

But something was very wrong.

Analysis of these transmissions indicated that the pacemaker battery was prematurely failing at a fast rate. To compound this problem, his family lived in a vast remote mountainous region of a western state. There was no cardiologist or appropriate pacemaker support equipment anywhere nearby to help this poor child. He was in a dangerous situation and could die!

I quickly made my boss and upper management aware of this serious problem. They were concerned, as was the Mayo Clinic. I did not get any directive or advice from my management. Nor was I told to do anything about this little boy's precarious condition.

"How insensitive of them," I thought. Were they simply treating this as one more thing to worry about? Or were they just assuming that somehow this problem would be solved. I saw it differently, since I too had an infant son who had been hospitalized. This little boy needed help as soon as possible. Screw management! That help had to come from me.

My family values kicked in. I owned this problem … it was mine to solve. Without a sense of urgency, this child could die.

Within two days, I had the Minnesota Air National Guard and a Mayo Clinic team readied to fly out and care for this child. He and his parents would be flown back to the Mayo Clinic and treated. He would live!

At the same time, Medtronic engineers were furiously scrambling to find out why the battery was failing so fast and if failure could be slowed or even reversed. Then came their revelation. The battery was not failing! While used for many years for telephone transmissions from earlier pacemaker models, the telephone transmission receiving instrument had never been tested for use with Spectrax. It could not properly assess how Spectrax pacemakers were working. Another set of transmissions to a newly-designed, quickly-assembled prototype telephone transmission receiving instrument confirmed their revelation. To my relief, the little boy was just fine!

Did this experience change Medtronic's process of developing new pacing products? It certainly did! The corporation recognized going forward that additional design considerations and testing were required to make sure that products used together actually worked properly together. The process of making sure that a group of products worked properly together subsequently evolved over the next few years ... and is now dubbed the "systems approach."

# Timing
# Is Everything

***What I Learned:*** *Sometimes circumstances allow you to take a big chance.*

During our first staff meeting, I learned that we were defaulting on a commitment made to the Atomic Energy Commission (now the Nuclear Regulatory Agency). In return for its help developing a nuclear-powered pacemaker, Medtronic promised to conduct a clinical study to keep track of all patients (and their pacemakers) until their death. This commitment was quite a challenge, since these nuclear-powered pacemakers were implanted in a relatively young population of patients who would each have to be followed for 10-20 years or more.

Medtronic went to great efforts to keep track of these patients. A concerted effort was made to find the lost ones, starting with calls made to the patients' referring and implanting physicians. We found some in jail. A few left their homes and returned to live on Indian reservations. Others moved to another community or retired abroad. Some were thought to be dead, but we found them to be alive. Our field staff visited many county government centers looking for death certificates of lost patients who might have died. More than a few deceased bodies were exhumed to confirm that the implanted pacemaker was among the remains.

Still, in spite of our best efforts, we were steadily losing track of a sizable number of patients and nuclear pacemakers.

The commission did not know how many patients were actually unaccounted for due to the vagueness of information we reported to them. We needed to tell the truth, before the problem grew worse. But I was worried that the Commission would impose harsh penalties, if we told them the truth. I did not know what or when to say anything, until an extremely newsworthy event occurred. While it was an extremely catastrophic event, it might provide a great chance to resolve our patient-tracking problem.

I contacted the Atomic Energy Commission and spoke with the staff member responsible for our nuclear-powered pacemaker study. Everything was disclosed … our efforts to locate patients and how many were lost. I pledged to keep looking for the lost patients and asked if that would be satisfactory.

"We are all extremely busy here right now. Just do the best you can," I was told.

That was exactly the type of response I had hoped for, knowing that the commission would be overwhelmed by the Three-Mile Island Nuclear Plant meltdown that had just occurred in Pennsylvania. I took advantage of this tragic event to chart a new, more reasonable course for the nuclear pacemaker study. Timing was everything!

# Squeezing Out a Decision

***What I Learned:*** *Creativity can be used to change the course of events. My best creativity training occurred in kindergarten. Training subsequently was spotty.*

"Too many cooks can spoil the broth," especially if they interpret the recipe differently. That was the case in 1980, when new regulations gave the Food and Drug Administration the responsibility to approve pending new medical device clinical research studies. After several weeks of meetings, the regulatory affairs and clinical research departments could not agree about how to respond to the new FDA regulations for a pending study. It would be our first study that required FDA approval to begin.

Complying with the new regulations was problematic for regulatory affairs due to their uncertainty about how to interpret the new regulations. They were reluctant to send any submission to the FDA seeking approval to start this study. It would set a precedence for what we could propose in the future.

I prepared and sent three different submissions about this pending clinical study. Regulatory affairs rejected all three. My divisional vice president told me that he was growing very tired of our inability to reach consensus. It was now past the date when the study was expected to begin.

A fresh approach was needed.

I decided to take advantage of the adage that "There is no such thing as a free lunch." I sent a new submission to regulatory affairs along with an invitation to a joint luncheon at a nearby restaurant to discuss it. The three key regulatory affairs staffers readily accepted my invitation and offer to drive.

I invited a key clinical research departmental staff member to join us and specifically instructed him to sit in the front passenger seat next to me. Doing so strategically placed my three regulatory guests uncomfortably squeezed together into the back seat of my small 1980 Honda Accord.

Cramped together, the five of us took off. But I had no intention of driving directly to any restaurant.

I acknowledged how crowded together they looked in the back seat as we drove along. Trying to be diplomatic about my seemingly bad decision to drive, they cracked forced smiles and nodded. From my perspective, I had laid a trap. I had temporarily kidnapped them. The ransom surfaced when I said, "We are not going to any restaurant until we reach agreement on my lastest submission. Was it acceptable?"

It took only a few minutes for me to get their acceptance. They wanted a few minor face-saving changes made. I readily agreed to them. Lunch was great.

Our FDA submission gained quick approval to conduct the next pending clinical study. To our collective credit, this submission served as an effective model for FDA submissions seeking FDA approval for many future clinical studies.

# Putting a Crack
# in The Glass Ceiling

**What I Learned:** *Doing the right thing can be risky.*
*It can also be rewarding.*

Quite unexpectedly, assigning two women to lead two different new high-technology clinical research studies created a dilemma. Both were middle-aged, skilled nurses who loved working in clinical research. Both understood the basics of pacemaker therapy. They were qualified and the only staff available to pursue these two projects.

I was obviously "clueless" when I made these assignments.

Shame on me for not knowing that staff females had only been allowed to lead "low" technology" clinical studies. I guess it had been assumed that women would not understand the complexities that high-technology pacing products posed. My boss, Nick Wartonick, was unaware of this practice. It probably had never been brought to his attention before.

Louise was a tall, quiet person with dark, straight, close-cut hair. When necessary though, she could easily take charge of any situation. I saw her as a natural leader who always gained the respect of those working with her. I asked Louise to lead a new pacemaker clinical research study. I knew she had good leadership skills, after she told me about her recent experience at a Central American hospital. She ran a nursing unit that was grossly understaffed. So, she had the healthier patients help care for the sicker ones. To me, that qualified her to lead a new, high-technology pacemaker clinical study.

After taking with some of his colleagues, my boss expressed some discomfort about Louise's new assignment. He backed off when I agreed to take full responsibility for this decision. While I was just kidding about it, he agreed to host my "farewell luncheon" if Louise failed. Admittedly, I was not totally sure Louise would be successful. But nothing I could think of told me otherwise.

Louise was not happy that I had assigned her to lead this study. It required her to learn much more details about how pacemakers worked, which she dreaded doing. But she did a great job leading the team that pursued this study. Her success put the first crack in the glass ceiling that kept women from visibly exerting their leadership skills at Medtronic, especially in technical matters.

I asked Nancy to lead a new pacemaker diagnostic Instrument study. Its use would help physicians know how to best adjust the settings for Medtronic's new family of "physiological" pacemakers.

Nancy was short and had a bubbly personality and curly blonde hair. Like Louise, she was upset that I had assigned to lead this clinical research study. Although I thought her pacing lead expertise qualified her to lead this pacemaker diagnostic instrument study, she was very hesitant to do so.

Nancy was hesitant because she knew nothing about this Instrument's new technology ... microprocessor control and software-based operation. She reluctantly accepted this assignment, knowing that a software engineer was assigned to work with her and provide technical support.

During the first test of the new Instrument, it froze. It stopped working during the pacemaker implant case. The software engineer frantically tried to get it to work. But he couldn't. Nancy suggested turning the Instrument off and then back on to get it to work. Reluctantly, he did so. To his amazement, it worked. Nancy was very proud of herself. Rightfully so! Her confidence shot up. She volunteered to cover the second implant case where the Instrument would be used by herself.

Nancy planned to catch the red-eye flight from Minneapolis to Washington D.C. Doing so would allow her to attend the second test of this diagnostic instrument early the next morning. She must have been distracted when she boarded the airplane. Nancy learned she had mistakenly boarded the wrong airplane, now flying to San Francisco. To her credit, she took another red-eye flight back from San Francisco to Washington D.C. She arrived in time to test the instrument during the scheduled pacemaker implant.

She did a great job on this project. She ultimately became recognized as a pacing lead expert. Like Louise, she too put a crack in the glass ceiling that kept women away from leading high technology projects. I was very proud of them. They both took a risk, knowing that I would support them any way I could if they had problems. I took great satisfaction in their accomplishments and Medtronic benefitted both times I took a chance!

Louise and Nancy were probably the first female employees to work on high-visibility, high-technology projects at Medtronic. Unknowingly, they helped open the doors for women to lead high-visibility, high-technology projects.

# A Giant Sequoia Towering Over Me

***What I Learned:*** *"If the shoe does not fit..." perhaps someone else should wear it.*

Deciding which U.S. physicians should participate as investigators in our clinical studies was challenging. My staff spent many hours in closed-door meetings with others to identify them. Heated discussions often erupted at some of these meetings. To be selected, a physician had to have some clinical research experience and be treating appropriate patients for pending clinical studies. Geographical location was also a factor, since they occasionally needed help from our field technical support staff.

Once selection was finalized, my clinical study managers officially invited these physicians to participate in their pending clinical studies. Physicians usually accepted immediately, since they were honored to have been selected or just liked being involved with new products. Our U.S. sales representatives were always informed when these invitations were made. But that was not the end of it.

Letting the sales organization know that we were selecting or had selected physicians for an upcoming clinical study was like "letting the genie out of the bottle." That's because some of our sales staff would encourage other physicians, their customers, to lobby us to become investigators. Sometimes they even promised them that they would become investigators. Once we invited physicians to be investigators, we could not accept other physicians on a study. If we did, that would offend those physicians whom we had already invited to participate in that study. Can you image how angry a physician would be if we withdrew their invitation to be a study investigator? These unsolicited encouragements and commitments were annoying, time-consuming and very disruptive.

The U.S. sales organization took no responsibility for problems this practice created. Rather, regional sales directors and district sales managers blamed my department each time they had to deal with the potential loss of a disillusioned customer, victimized by this practice. These problems were why I got so many nasty, almost hateful telephone calls from the sales organization starting on my first day as clinical research director.

More than once I was told what I could do with the department ... not anything I dare repeat. It was scary anytime a U.S. regional sales director or district sales manager caught me in the hallway or came to my office specifically to express their anger. Every one of them was much taller than me, very upset and border-line physically threatening. I pictured them as a giant sequoia, bending over to look me in the eye while venting. They did not hesitate to use a lot of profanity to express their feelings.

Something had to be done to manage this dilemma. Merely reacting to it did not work!

I developed a simple approach to manage how physicians would be selected to participate in our clinical studies. My clinical study manager and development team would identify about half of them. The sales organization were allowed to identify the remaining ones, all under the direction of the district sales managers and regional sales directors. That approach allowed me to shift the problem of raising false expectations away from my staff and direct it back toward the sales organization where it belonged.

It worked! Heated meetings convened to determine how to handle unsolicited commitments morphed into social gatherings. Staunch adversaries became close colleagues. Once, I even had to remind them to take a few minutes to select the physicians needed for an upcoming study.

One regional sales director summed up the results best. During a chance meeting, he acknowledged: "I now understand the need to limit how many physicians can participate in a clinical study. I'm very dissatisfied that I must make difficult choices to exclude some valued customers (physicians) in my region. But I know the other three regional sales directors have to make the same decisions. So I'm ok with the process, since I know you're treating us all equally."

# The Patients Who Died

**What I Learned**: *Get all the facts you can, before conveying anything substantial ... good or bad.*

K en Barton was technically astute and had a warm, inviting personality. He readily accepted serving as a clinical study manager for our physiological pacemaker clinical studies. Medtronic invested heavily in physiological pacemakers, since they offered the potential to substantially improve the quality of life of patients using this pacing therapy. Physiological pacemaker sales could be expected to boost corporate revenues considerably, if the outcomes of these studies were positive. Therefore, many corporate executives were kept apprised about how these studies were going.

Early in the main physiological pacemaker study, Ken learned that four or five patients died at one major research center. A patient death was usually a rare event in any pacemaker clinical study. But four or five deaths in a short period of time at one center was a major concern. What if these pacemakers somehow caused these deaths! Ken immediately called the clinical research physician at this center. He asked about the deaths and if the pacemakers were involved in them. He got more information how the patients died, but nothing about pacemaker involvement.

Ken consulted with me before telling others about so many deaths. Unless pacemaker involvement was ruled out, we knew there would be corporate-wide major doubts about their safety. We decided that he should first talk to these patients' nurse before communicating anything to others. He had a look of relief when he walked into my office about an hour later to report his conversation with her. She told him that the patients were all expected to die soon. The doctor implanted the pacemakers anyway, just to see if they could help. The pacemakers worked properly, but unfortunately the patients died soon after each implant. No message of alarm had to be conveyed to the corporation. What a relief!

# Do You Remember Those Cases?

***What I Learned:*** *Humor does not have to be very funny to be effective. Sometimes just a little dose will do. It can be far more effective than sarcasm to defuse a difficult situation.*

A substantial effort was made to train physicians how to use Medtronic's newest products. I and others were often recruited to provide many one-on-one training sessions for visiting physicians. Of my many training sessions, I recall only one. It was with a cardiac surgeon.

He was an elderly man, impeccably dressed in a dark blue suit. Unlike most surgeons, he was soft-spoken and very mild-mannered. That was in contrast to the brash and somewhat arrogant young cardiac surgeons I worked with in the past.

Our training session was scheduled to last one hour. He readily grasped my instructions about how to implant our new physiological pacemaker and its pacing leads. But teaching him how to adjust the pacemaker settings was very problematic, because the electronic heart simulator given to me for this part of the training was not working properly.

"Why me? Why was I given a faulty simulator?" I asked myself.

As I continued to struggle with the faulty simulator, I could tell he was becoming impatient with me and the training session. Nothing I tried worked. I could not wait until it was over. To his credit, he offered some supportive comments, as I fiddled and fiddled with the simulator. Finally, I gave up.

"How could I diplomatically end this humiliating session?" I wondered. A way of doing so came to me.

"Doctor. Do you ever have cases that do not turn out well?" I asked.

"Oh. Yes," he responded.

He readily agreed with my contention that, "I bet those are the cases you never forget, especially the most difficult ones" He nodded his head in complete agreement.

He laughed after I exclaimed, "Well doctor, I am not going to forget this training session for a long, long time." I abruptly ended the session, but I never forgot it.

# New Type of Vice President

***What I Learned:*** *It is hard to be successful without creating some serious problems along the way. Some problems you create "can't be put back into the bottle."*

I still vividly recall two requests made directly to me about physicians becoming investigators. The first came from a Canadian sales representative. He told me that one of his customers complained that his colleagues did not respect him. This physician thought he would gain their respect, if we would make him a clinical researcher in one of our studies.

We needed another Canadian researcher in one study and this particular physician was well-qualified to assume this role. So, this was an easy request to accommodate. I wrote the physician and personally invited him to join a clinical research study. As I wrote, I kept thinking about the Wizard of Oz story. "I am granting him respect," I thought, "just like the Wizard would have done."

The other request was very problematic. It came from a corporate executive from another division. He wanted a very prominent cardiologist to be a clinical researcher on an upcoming, high-visibility pacemaker study. This corporate executive was well-liked throughout Medtronic and known to be quite persuasive. At the time, he led the field technical support organization that my staff relied upon, when physicians

122

around the country needed technical support with our clinical study pacing products.

Medtronic had already designated this particular cardiologist as a "Key Opinion Leader," so it made sense to include him in this study. If he participated in a study and the pacing product study results were positive, he likely would strongly advocate use of that new product at medical meetings or when conversing with colleagues. Obtaining direct experience with the new pacing product through participation in a clinical study would add credibility to any advocacy.

But there were two compelling reasons to deny this request. He had a history of publicly criticizing any product he did not like, even if his views were unfounded or it was about a problem that already had been corrected. Of greater concern was his poor compliance track record in clinical research. He did not always comply with clinical study protocol requirements. Getting him to return clinical study data was often problematic.

New FDA regulations required us to report these compliance problems to them. He would definitely be embarrassed by our reports to the FDA about him. If the FDA thought the problems were severe. they could terminate him as a researcher. Medtronic's "Key Opinion Leader" could become a "Key Opinion Detractor," bad-mouthing Medtronic publicly at every occasion possible. Such compliance problems might make the FDA question the validity of our clinical studies and impose tough regulatory or legal action.

The corporate executive understood the potential problems his request created. But he was relentless. After I firmly denied his request, he convened a meeting with me, my boss Nick and our division's vice president.

No consensus was reached at this meeting. The decision to include or exclude this cardiologist was left entirely up to me. Out of frustration, I subsequently proposed in jest an absurd solution. Knowing that this cardiologist practiced in New York City, I proposed having him implant the clinical study pacing products in international waters, just beyond New York City aboard the U.S. Hope. The U.S. Hope was a decommissioned U.S. Navy hospital ship that offered free medical care and training around the world.

I suggested donating ten thousand dollars to Project Hope to make the ship available for these implants. Some at Medtronic were intrigued by this unusual possibility, since the FDA would not have any jurisdiction in international waters. This scenario could allow the cardiologist to participate in the clinical study. Naturally, this possibility never materialized. It was not practical and was legally questionable. While it was an absolutely absurd proposal, I pretended to be disappointed that it was turned down.

Still, the corporate executive persisted. Out of continued frustration and, in hindsight, poor judgment. I took the next step. I wrote a memo to this executive about his request and circulated it widely. After delicately re-explaining the problems we could face, I left the decision up to him. "I would agree to add this cardiologist to our clinical research study, if he would agree to be the Vice President in Charge of Going to Jail." He never answered my memo and the cardiologist never participated in any study.

Was that the end of this saga? No, it was not. The ramification of my memo came back to haunt me about a year or so later when this corporate executive became my boss.

# But Daddy ...

**What I Learned:** *Very little is required to show a big interest in someone.*

I happened to see Tim Lathrop talking to his young son one day. His son proudly showed him a gold star he earned from his teacher on a picture he drew. Tim congratulated his son, reached into his pocket and gave him a quarter as a reward. It was a special moment between a parent and a child.

I remembered this special moment a few weeks later when I reviewed the first draft of Tim's Spectrax Clinical Study Report. I made a relatively large number of editorial changes and comments in red ink throughout the report. Since I remembered the special moment when Tim praised his son's drawing, I printed "Great Job" in big bold letters and pasted a large red star I bought specifically for this occasion on the title page. Would Tim show it to his son? How would his son react?

Tim told me about his son's response to seeing "Great Job" and the star on the title page. His son gave Tim a nickel from his piggy bank and praised Tim. But he became confused when he looked through Tim's report. "Daddy," he asked "how come you got a red star when you made so many mistakes?'

Tim was very pleased that I remembered this touching incident. He took great delight in telling others what happened after his son saw his report.

# Hallelujah

***What I Learned:*** *How your day ends is far more important than how it begins.*

A company-sponsored week in Hawaii was awarded to those of us who participated in the Spectrax Clinical Research Study. Such an award was very rare, possibly the first time Medtronic recognized the success of any department or clinical research study. The study results launched Spectrax into a highly successful marketing campaign. Spectrax sales were boosting the Medtronic's bottom line, since it substantially improved the lives of patient recipients. The study results also cemented my department's transformation from a perceived liability to an acknowledged asset.

The trip itinerary had the obligatory educational sessions. But it was mostly packed with many desirable activities paid for by the Company. Earle Bakken, Medtronic's co-founder and Chairman of the Board, would be our host for this week. Each of us was invited to bring a guest. I looked forward to this trip with my wife. Perhaps it would sooth our rocky relationship.

A sunset ocean dinner cruise was held on the second or third night in Hawaii. About thirty of us boarded the Hallelujah, which was moored in a bay on the Big Island. While there were storm warnings for later that night, the sun was shining and the waters were calm in that bay. Once we left land, the waters became choppy. Undaunted, we headed out to sea.

Thirty minutes later, we were in big trouble. The sky darkened as our casual dining cruise turned into a scary ride. The Hallelujah was crawling up and then careening down larger and larger waves. Suddenly we saw a huge wave heading toward us. It was large enough to break over the entire boat. Most of us were on deck, except for a few in the steering cabin with the captain. We hung on to whatever we could for dear life. I honestly thought my life was over when that wave hit and the sea momentarily engulfed us.

We miraculously survived this first huge wave only to see another large one heading toward us. It was not as large as the first wave, but still it broke over half of the boat. I looked up quickly after the second wave to see what happened to those trapped inside the steering cabin. It had momentarily filled up from floor to ceiling with sea water, since I could see it rapidly emptying.

It was really scary. I did not think our boat could sustain another large wave. But another wave like the two that struck us never came.

Hallelujah! We were lucky to have survived. There were rough seas on the way back to shore, but no huge waves. No one slept well that night. With great hesitation, I joined two others the next day on a deep-sea fishing trip. We caught a large mahi-mahi that everyone ate for dinner that night.

# I Found a Table

**What I Learned:** *Feign strength when you have weakness, especially if you have little to lose.*

When my clinical research department was moved into new offices, I was not given a table and chairs for my new office. I needed them to hold informal meetings there. My periodic calls to corporate facilities about getting them were frustrating. The only response I got was something like "You'll get them soon." After months of trying, I could not even get a commitment about when I could expect to get a table and chairs. One morning I decided to take control of this problem.

I called corporate facilities and told them that I no longer needed a table and chairs. Instead, my staff would help me get a table I found on the outdoor patio just outside the cafeteria. Then with my best theatrical expression, I described the table as "... a wonderful six-foot round green metal table with built-in benches and a striped umbrella. It has a lovely shade of green, my favorite color. The white and green striped umbrella will look just great in my office."

Amazingly, I got a table and chairs a few hours later.

# Accounting Needs a Receipt

***What I Learned:*** *I took a graduate accounting course to learn how to think like and negotiate with accountants. And it paid off!*

I asked my staff to work late on a very important project that had to be completed that night. Since it would take hours to complete it, I ordered a pizza dinner for us.

Because I personally paid for dinner, I knew accounting would need a receipt to get reimbursed for this expense. But the pizza guy did not bring a receipt with him. Nor did he have any blank receipts in his car. Since it was 20 degrees below zero that frozen night, I didn't have the heart to ask him to get me a receipt from the restaurant.

Wanting to get reimbursed and needing a receipt to get it, I improvised.

I stapled all three pizza boxes to my monthly expense report. It was the best smelling expense report and the only one like it that anyone in accounting could ever remember. And I got reimbursed.

# Before There Was E-Mail and Text Messaging

***What I Learned:*** *My best creative ideas occurred to me outside of the workplace.*

Nick Wartonick was a great boss. He was a soft-spoken, easy going Air Force Reserve Lieutenant Colonel. I greatly appreciated his trust in me to steer the clinical research department in unchartered waters. When I occasionally needed to confer briefly with our division's senior vice president, Nick gave me permission to do so without needing his approval or review beforehand.

Getting a meeting to confer with this vice president was impossible, since he was always busy ... even for a five-minute meeting. While shaving, I thought of a way to gain access to him involving his secretary.

I knew his secretary well enough to ask for help. She agreed to help me, presumably since I always expressed appreciation for what she and others did to help me. I took an interest in anyone I worked with. That is how my father treated his employees, and they loved him.

In return for this secretary's help, I would maintain her supply of Mountain Dew.

I'd call her if I needed a few minutes of her boss' time. She would then call to tell me when he was headed to the restroom. I'd go directly to that restroom and got a few minutes of quality time with him. Since we were conversing while voiding in nearby urinals, I called it "U-mail."

The vice president never knew that our five or six impromptu urinal conversations were orchestrated occurrences. Accounting never knew, since I was pretty sure I could not submit any Mountain Dew bill as a "Meeting Expense." Such an unusual expense certainly would have turned a few heads, even though they allowed me to have very time-efficient, highly productive meetings. Can you imagine the array of memos that corporate human resources might issue about impromptu bathroom meetings?

# This Year Budgeting Will Be Easier

***What I Learned:*** *Time spent budgeting is far from a company's finest hour. Hallmark should offer sympathy cards to give to those who have to budget. A twelve-step program could be established to support them during budgeting.*

Our division's vice president of finance readily acknowledged that last year's budgeting process was very complex and time consuming. It was the first time I went through budgeting at Medtronic. I had to rework my proposed budget three times. Each time I had to provide endless details to seek the resources needed to pursue all projects planned for the upcoming fiscal year. While I disliked the process, it eventually ended. I got all major planned projects funded.

Then the new fiscal year began. A few weeks into the first new quarter I became very cynical about budgeting. That's because once the new fiscal year began, I and all other managers had to delay any planned new hiring or expenditures. The corporation sought this delay until it could confirm that its planned first quarter revenues would materialize. No new projects could be started. Work on on-going projects had to be curtailed. To make matters worse, several unplanned clinical projects arose that had to be pursued as aggressively as the planned projects. Upper management essentially bound our hands for almost three months. Even though we lost three months by limiting our activities, we still had to "pull a rabbit out of a hat" and complete all projects on time and within budget for the new fiscal year.

My cynicism changed into indifference toward the end of that fiscal year. I promised myself that I was not going to take my second budgeting process very seriously.

Experience taught me that unplanned projects could be expected. So, I added a funding provision for unplanned projects in my first proposed budget for the next fiscal year. While I had a good rationale for taking this approach, I did not worry about this funding being denied. Instead, I would rely upon what I learned in an accounting course I took to understand corporate finances better.

I started presenting my department as a "business unit," by noting something new in my monthly progress reports to upper management. I began reporting sales revenues Medtronic gained when physicians ordered pacing products to implant in our clinical research studies. I recall that the first dollar amount was approximately $500,000 (circa 1980).

The first time my boss Nick wanted us to pursue an unplanned, non-budgeted project during the new fiscal year, I agreed to take it on. But I made it conditional upon reducing the number of pacemakers or pacing leads that would be used in our planned clinical research projects. Because Medtronic did not want to lose these sales revenues, this approach worked the few times I used it. Nick was always able to get me the extra funds needed for any unplanned project. He was able to do so, since the funds I sought were always far less than the lost revenues would be.

I achieved my objective. Budgeting was simple and easy, as it also was for the following fiscal year with a new boss ... my last one as director of clinical research.

# Don't Do That Again

***What I Learned:*** *It's a blessing to have a boss with some sense of humor.*

I was startled twice while talking on the telephone. Both times my in-basket contents suddenly fell onto my head. It was symbolic of the deluge of marginally useless information being sent to me (and others) to read. I saw a need to draw attention to the corporate-wide practice of over-communicating. Knowing my boss had a sense of humor, I started citing the "IBH factor" in my monthly reports to him. He, in turn, passed on the "IBH factor" in his monthly reports to upper management.

Three months later, he asked me to explain what IBH was; people throughout the corporation were asking him about it. Whatever it was, he knew it had doubled during the last few months. It went from a little over four inches to almost ten inches during the three months I was reporting it.

Keep in mind it was 1980, before pagers, e-mails and text messages existed. Everything was hard copy. I told him that IBH stood for "In-Basket Height." IBH stood for the height of memos, notices, trade journals and other materials in my in-basket at the end of each month. I was receiving an excessive amount of materials to read.

Nick's directives were always mild-mannered. Sometimes they were sprinkled with a little dry, but enjoyable, sense of good humor. After hearing what IBH meant, he cracked a small smile. Then ever so calmly he told me, "Don't do that again." I agreed not to report IBH factor again.

But the amount of materials I was getting was rapidly increasing. So, I started reporting how much the materials in my in-box weighed. I recall a weight of 22.0 pounds after two months. Of this amount, 21.5 pounds was (in today's vernacular) "junk mail." In today's business world, I would have reported "NET," the number of e-mails and text messages.

# Phantom of the Second Floor

***What I Learned:*** *When all else fails, try a little humor.*

One comment in one of my monthly reports attracted a lot of interest. I simply asked if the "Phantom of the Second Floor" would please return my staff's telephone calls and messages to him. If this request was not effective, my plan was to personally steal his office telephone. To me, that would be an appropriate course of action. From my perspective, he wasn't using it anyway.

I got telephone calls from many directors and vice presidents, asking if that person worked for them. After I named this person during one call, he promptly started returning all calls my staff made to him.

# I'll Give You a Ride

***What I Learned:*** *Sometimes you can only do so much to correct a difficult situation.*

Our second departmental secretary was a delightful, older employee ... very personable, incredibly loyal and willing to tackle anything. Until recently, her professional career had many positive highlights. But lately, keeping up with a hectic schedule and pressing workload became more and more difficult for her. Unfortunately, she often made mistakes that created big problems for me and my staff.

If asked, she would find a way for me to meet with the President of the United States. But she could not always staple a three-page memo together in the right order. On several meeting invitations, she cited the correct meeting date but the wrong meeting time.

We both knew that she needed to find another job, one that could accommodate her abilities and shortcomings. Given her age and other personal factors, I was not allowed to fire her. That would have been hard to do anyway, since I truly liked her and understood why she had problems. Rather, I was told to show patience and give her plenty of time to find another job elsewhere in our division. But that was impossible. Her reputation for making mistakes was widely known throughout our division and elsewhere within our building.

She needed to find a job in another facility. Since she did not drive, I did what any one in my position might have done. I drove her to interviews in other divisions.

She never got another job, and reluctantly accepted a generous offer to retire a year or so early.

# Those Small Signs
# Are Important

**What I Learned:** *Even the simplest things can be missed, when you are preoccupied.*

I ignored the first obvious sign that I was in the wrong place ... pink walls. I recall thinking, "How unusual to see two tampon dispensers on the wall." Still, no red flag went off in my mind. I was focused on finding a urinal quickly to urgently relieve my overly filled bladder. Only after not finding one anywhere did I realize my mistake. It could have been more embarrassing, if anyone else was in that women's restroom!

It only took a few seconds to realize that I made the same mistake again months later. Unlike the first time, the restroom was full of women. I left immediately once someone screamed, "Frank. What are you doing here?"

To this day, I always make it a point to read those small signs posted outside the restrooms. I read them very carefully.

# Corporate Blinders

**What I Learned:** Accepting that something can go wrong begins with imagining that it could.

R ace horses wear blinders to see only what is ahead of them. Corporate executives unknowingly put on blinders sometimes that cloud their judgement. Corporate blinders make it hard to consider all the consequences of a decision they were asked to make. I had to seek a decision from the executive I invited to be the "Vice President of Going to Jail" about three important clinical study issues. One decision was sought before he became my new boss. The other two decisions occurred shortly after he became my new boss. In my opinion, he wore corporate blinders on each occasion.

Medtronic's new family of physiological pacemakers each added a new pacing therapy to those already in wide-spread use. The earliest versions of this new physiological pacing therapy relied upon sensing the heart's S-A Node (sino-atrial) … a group of heart cells that normally make the heart beat faster or slower. Unlike all other pacemaker models, the use of S-A Node sensing allowed the pacemaker to know when the patient's heart should be beating faster or slower and if any beats would be missing then. If so, the pacemaker would stimulate the heart to prevent any beats from being skipped.

Knowing that a variety of S-A Node diseases existed, I surveyed physicians who had implanted and evaluated a new physiological pacemaker in our clinical studies.

I asked them to estimate the percent of S-A Nodes in their physiological pacemaker patients that functioned normally after one year. They reported a 10 percent loss of normal S-A Node function per year. Such a loss did not make physiological pacemakers unsafe. Rather, it meant the heart's ability to change heart rate without missing any beats would be gradually lost along with any quality of life improvement expected from this new pacing therapy.

I thought it was our ethical duty to report these findings to physicians. I wanted them to know that these pacemakers could not be relied upon for long-term physiological pacing. After reviewing my report, a colleague suggested that I ask this corporate executive to review it. He disliked it, refuting its findings. He strongly advised me not to disseminate it. Given his widely acclaimed corporate stature, I reluctantly agreed not to do so. Later, I regretted not disseminating it. It was the only time I remember not following my mother's sage advice to "always do the right thing."

I never understood why he took this stance. Possibly it was because he knew that future physiological pacemaker designs would not have to rely solely upon normal S-A node function for their operation. In retrospect, it could have been poor judgement or lack of insight. It could also have been that he was protecting the highly acclaimed physiological pacing brand image in marketing promotions. While my research findings were subsequently confirmed, they did not erase my regret for not disseminating these findings.

The second decision involved the outcome of Nancy's diagnostic instrument clinical study. While this study's findings were generally favorable, it identified a substantial instrument shortcoming. It failed to detect a cardiac condition that could make physiological pacing dangerous for some patients. I was alarmed about this finding!

I was utterly shocked by my boss' response about the instrument's shortcoming ... like unexpectedly being sucker-punched! Rather than being thankful that this shortcoming was identified or asking my opinion about it, he gave me two options about this study and my bonus relating to it.

I could approve the study as completed and not recommend any Instrument changes. Doing so would allow it to be immediately released for sale according to the business plan. Or, I could recommend changes to correct this shortcoming. Correcting it would delay sales and cost me my bonus for completing this project on schedule. This time I followed my mother sage advice. I chose the latter option and lost a substantial part of my bonus that year.

I felt betrayed as a clinical research professional. Wasn't finding out if a new product was safe part of my job? If so, why was I penalized for doing my job?

A more critical example of corporate blinders began with anecdotal reports of premature polyurethane insulation failure in pacing leads. A staff colleague and I felt obligated to re-evaluate this polyurethane insulation. We wanted to learn how often and when failures were occurring. If the potential for failure was high, knowing so early could head off bigger problems with polyurethane leads. Regrettably, our clinical studies only followed polyurethane pacing lead patients for three months ... not enough time for insulation failures to occur. Out of a sense of duty, we planned a simple clinical study to check the insulation status of several hundred pacing leads after being implanted for one year. It could be accomplished for about $5,000, a very small amount compared to what our other studies cost.

But my boss struck it from my budget. He did not think it was worthwhile to pursue this research and said no. That was a big mistake!

Polyurethane insulation failures were very evident a year later. If pursued, our study might have limited the number of polyurethane lead implants to a few thousand. Instead, a few patients died and tens of thousands of polyurethane leads had to be recalled. Many depositions were needed for the legal actions that followed. The Food and Drug Administration imposed penalties that took years to overcome.

Fate made me the right person with the right idea at the right time. But none of that mattered.

That colleague and I met for lunch a few times after he left Medtronic. While we worked together on many Medtronic clinical research studies, we only really talked about one … the polyurethane pacing lead insulation study that never happened.

Later, I reluctantly concluded that Medtronic was not always a shining example of how to deal with product problems. I understand that medical device company executives must consider many factors when a potential or actual safety problem arises. Rather than shooting the messenger, perhaps a key question should be asked when problems arise: "What would you do if one the patients involved was your own mother?"

# The Beginning of the End

***What I Learned:*** *Anxiety is often far worse than reality.*

I regretted losing Nick as my boss. Regrettably, the relationship with my new boss began with me inviting him to be the "Vice President in Charge of Going to Jail." While I disagreed with his three "corporate blinder" decisions, I was committed to make our relationship work!

There were good reasons to be optimistic about my fate. He was respectful and showed some interest in my ideas and plans for the department. He usually greeted me with a big smile, a signature trademark of his friendly persona. He did not ask me to change anything we were doing. He even encouraged me to seek out and maintain closes ties with individuals who might make good future departmental staff members. Weren't these good signs?

Still, my gut told me that something was wrong in our relationship. Little things that happened made me anxious. I started losing confidence about keeping my job. I felt like an unwanted dandelion, slowly losing my seeds of confidence due to barely perceptible winds of uncertainty.

The straw that broke the camel's back was that our management styles differed. He loved telling other executives interesting little tidbits about on-going clinical research. That meant he wanted to know excruciating details about every on-going clinical study. But I rarely knew much to tell my boss. The only time I knew details was if one of my study managers sought my help about a major problem. Doing so allowed me to devote most of my time to make sure my staff was successful. In retrospect, I failed to recognize the importance of accommodating my boss' need for study details ... things to gossip about.

Eventually, I sought a colleague's advice when my anxiety grew too pervasive to ignore. The advice was good, but hard to swallow. Asking my boss about my fate would not change his mind. Knowing I lost my job might be better than living with the anxiety about possibly losing it. I'd stop worrying about what might happen. I would "get back on track" and do what I needed to do professionally and personally.

When I asked, I got good news and bad. Unfortunately, I would have to immediately leave my position. That would allow someone else to experience being Director of Clinical Research. At least that's what I was told. In return, I would become a corporate consultant for one year. While consulting, it would be my responsibility to find a permanent job within Medtronic. That was my fate, not my choice!

While I was extremely disheartened, at least I had a temporary job and a reasonable amount of time to find a new, permanent one.

I did learn a valuable lesson from this experience. Anxiety can be far worse than reality. Worrying about something bad that might happen raises an unending number of vexing questions that have no answers. Your mind fills with uncertainty. Once I accepted that a devastating event occurred, I could then focus on what I had to do in the near future to overcome it. I did "get back in the race" and it paid off!

# Lovers
# Who Wander

**What I Learned:** *While it can be hurtful, the painful truth is sometimes necessary to know.*

Ideally, we rely upon four sets of building blocks to create sound structure in our lives: a good job, a supportive family, sound finances and healthy personal relationships. My structure was crumbling not just because I had lost a good job. I no longer enjoyed being a parent to my now adolescent kids … a chemically dependent son and a very rebellious daughter. Both were living with me, since their mother threw them out. Supporting two households ate away at my financial security.

I had to deal with one of my wife's relatives who was dedicated to helping her during our divorce proceedings. These proceeding should have been simple and quick. Once he started "helping," the divorce proceedings became complex and protracted. He never missed a chance to complicate my life. My married friends mostly chose to side with my wife and abandoned me.

I found myself in a sea of uncertainty, searching for calmer waters.

Other than good health, a good relationship with an attractive, interesting woman was now the sole positive thing in my life. This seemingly loving relationship was a great source of comfort and support, except for a few events that planted doubt in my mind. Then, I accidentally found out that ours was not the monogamous relationship I thought it was.

The only structured thing in my life was gone ... shattered!

I know that I was not the first person in a committed relationship, where cheating occurred. Back in the '50s, Dion sang "Lovers Who Wander." His song vividly tells how love is lost when infidelity creeps in. But it never touched on the heartache and devastation the resulting fall-out produces.

I walked away from someone I cared for deeply. While I never purposely sought another soul mate, someone wonderful later came into my life just by chance. She proposed to me ... and I accepted!

# Dear IRS ...

**What I Learned:** *Sometimes being creative involves using a little humor to solve a problem.*

Of dozens of joint Federal Tax Returns filed over the years, I only remember one. I do not remember it, because we owed so much or got a huge refund. I recall it with a smile and a chuckle, because of how I dealt with a glaring omission in this return

I was going through a nasty divorce. My attempts at being conciliatory went on deaf ears. I was nearly broke due to lawyer fees, supporting two residences and having two problematic children living me.

It was imperative to file a joint tax return to get a refund of several thousand dollars to pay for some of these expenses. But ultimately my wife refused to sign the joint return my accountant prepared. I did not want to lose it, by having to file a single return. With no savings and only a few hundred dollars in my checking account, I was rapidly draining my retirement funds to pay bills. I needed that refund.

"Desperate times call for desperate measures." So, I tried a "Hail Mary." Football fans know it as the last desperate play of the game. While its odds of success are extremely low, it is absolutely the last and only chance of winning the game.

I sent in our joint Federal Tax Return without my wife's signature. A brief note attached to it would hopefully persuade the IRS to accept this joint tax return. The note read:

"Dear IRS,

My wife and I are going through a nasty divorce. She refuses to sign this return, because she is very mad at me. I truly hope that you accept this filing without question.

Feel free to pass this note around to your colleagues when on coffee break or during lunch. Like you, I'm sure that they will see the humor in it.

Frank Freedman"

The return was accepted without question ... thank goodness.

# Corporate Purgatory

*What I Learned: Regardless of your circumstances, how you use your time is the biggest gamble you can make in your life. That's why I rarely gamble.*

I did not obtain many projects to work on during my one-year stint as a corporate consultant. None came from anyone in my division. I took a few self-improvement courses to fill some free time I had at Medtronic.

I asked some colleagues to complete a survey about me for one of these courses. The survey indicated that they viewed me as someone who made "important" contributions to Medtronic. I attributed their response more to my corporate-looking dress attire, than to the occasional consulting work I was doing.

While I applied for many open positions at Medtronic, I never got past any screening interview with the human resource representative. I was highly qualified to assume these positions and enjoyed a good reputation throughout Medtronic. However, no hiring manager interviewed me. That was a bad sign.

I viewed my Medtronic existence as being in "Corporate Purgatory" … stuck where I did not want to be and not knowing any way out. I was spending a lot of time trying to find a new job without any success.

Had my boss black-listed me? It certainly seemed so. If he was angry with me about that memo, he sure kept it well-concealed. Still, he did make me leave my director's job. Was he now making sure no one in the Corporation would hire me?

Possibly being black-listed while trying to find a job was just one pressing problem I faced. There were others that took considerable time to address. I was in the midst of nasty divorce proceedings, struggling to parent two problematic adolescents living with me (and a third living with her mother) and $200 away from being bankrupt. I never knew when some new pressing personal issue would arise. And arise they did.

There were documents to prepare for my attorney to file, depositions and court appearances. I dealt with many in our school district about my children's behavior on a regular basis. It took time to prepare for the many interviews I had. I took them seriously, since I needed to find another job at Medtronic.

Instead of letting adversities overwhelm me while in "purgatory," I gradually learned how to deal with them during my last year at Medtronic.

At first, it was hard to concentrate on anything. I could not even enjoy casual conversations with close, supportive colleagues. My mind was always awhirl with agonizing questions about my circumstances that had no answers. A glass or two of wine before bedtime was the usual reason I slept during the first few weeks in purgatory. I was in crisis mode! But I owned this nightmare and had to deal with it. It was mine to fix, not to dwell on. I had to "… pick myself up and get back in the race," and I did.

I gradually adopted a helpful attitude about getting through each day, when I took time to look at myself. I pictured myself as a machine, grinding away continuously to complete one task after another. The picture I saw was a previously well-oiled machine that was rapidly wearing out trying to accomplish a never-ending number of tasks each day. My thinking changed. I started viewing myself as a human being with strengths and limitations. I needed to step back from the craziness and craft a survival plan.

I had always kept a list of everything I had to do, updating it often. But I began to realize that it was more than just a list of things to do. I could rely on it to for assurance that I knew everything I had to do. That was part of my survival plan, because it allowed me to stop worrying if I forgot about needing to do something important. The other part of my survival plan involved making sure the list was current each day before work. After prioritizing items on this list, I would then decide what I would work on that day. By considering my time constraints. I stopped feeling guilty about the things I did not get done. After all, I was only human and not a machine.

I also tried to schedule some activity each day that I would enjoy. It could be playing tennis, reading a book, having coffee with a friend or something else. Time was certainly a precious commodity. Taking "me time" for such an activity was a good investment in myself. It gave me a much-needed balance in my life. Because we humans are constantly pulled in many directions, I was able to achieve good balance about 80 percent of the time.

If at all possible, I wanted to find another job at Medtronic. I thought it would be easier to continue working there than starting over somewhere else. As much as I wanted a Medtronic job, I abruptly terminated what became my last job interview there. From the tone of his remarks during the interview, I could tell that, once again, I would not get this or any job I sought in the Company. The light bulb in my brain had finally turned on. I shocked myself and the human resources representative by suddenly standing up and exclaiming, "This interview is over."

A colleague arranged for me to continue my employment for an additional three months. I would work as a regulatory affairs consultant to prepare a complex FDA submission seeking approval to conduct a clinical study for a new type of pacemaker therapy. That three-month project was a gift. It allowed me to update my regulatory submission skills, which I relied upon in many, many future professional endeavors. It was a great example of that time-tested adage: "God does not close one door without opening another."

# Corporate
# Russian Roulette

**What I Learned:** *A door rarely closes in life without another one opening up. The trick is to look for the opened door.*

I used project management to obtain regulatory and technical information from individuals throughout the Company for this complex FDA submission. It was the first use of project management for any regulatory affairs submission at Medtronic. And it worked well. Regulatory affairs departments across the Corporation subsequently adopted project management. They used it to gather information from contributing ad hoc team members and gain their assistance to prepare their submissions.

Unexpectedly, I obtained FDA approval very quickly. I posted many notes and letters of commendation for this accomplishment on my office walls. No one thought FDA approval of my submission was possible, since some key supporting information was lacking and this new therapy was truly revolutionary. Not only did I get approval, I got it in only 30 days. To my knowledge, that record accomplishment for a new type of pacing therapy stood the test of time at Medtronic for many years.

But the most prominent posting in my office was a letter from my boss officially terminating my employment in one week. It came immediately after I got the approval. I temporarily relished my accomplishment, a roller coaster "high," knowing that I would be leaving Medtronic very soon.

Whether by design or not, one week did not provide enough time to arrange a celebratory event for the approval I obtained. Nor did it provide enough time to arrange an event where I could say goodbye to colleagues. My continued presence was embarrassing for my boss, since many colleagues publicly expressed their dismay about my termination. While that was extremely gratifying, I still needed a job.

I had two memorable encounters during my last week at Medtronic. One was with a new employee I knew from years earlier when I was a volunteer at her non-profit organization. She sought my advice about working in a corporation. I coined the phrase "Corporate Russian Roulette" to frame the advice I gave her.

"Always look out for yourself. You can be a happy, productive employee who has a great relationship with your boss. Then something happens and you get a new boss. Being his or her employee just does not work out. Whether it's the new boss' constant micromanagement style, a personality clash or a conflicting set of values ... you're out of a job." I felt sad that I had to give this type of advice.

I also had a chance encounter with Earle Bakken, Medtronic's co-founder and board member. He made it a point to know me and many, many other employees. Earle mentioned having recently met my son, who was his waiter at a Medtronic-sponsored dinner that Earl hosted. That was indicative of the interest he took in everyone he knew. What a truly wonderful guy Earle was.

Earle knew I had been terminated. He was sad that I was leaving and wished me well. I wanted to tell him how angry I was about being terminated. But I had too much respect for him to say anything like that. So I said goodbye and whole-heartedly thanked him for my years at Medtronic, especially the first six (of seven) years. There we were ... two men genuinely fond of each other ... wishing each other the best while standing side by side at adjacent urinals.

A few years later when I started my own consulting business, Earle gave me a great endorsement about my Medtronic successes. I printed his endorsement prominently on my first company brochure. As far as I know, no one else was ever successful in getting that type of reference from Earle. That endorsement helped me tremendously when I began my consulting career a few years later.

# AFTERWORD

A severance package kept me on the payroll for several months after I left Medtronic. One senior executive commented at a meeting and later in writing that, "… married men make good managers." While hurtful to hear because I was getting a divorce, that comment gave me solid basis to seek severance pay. I did not have to claim I was "wrongfully terminated," a common practice then.

Regrettably, none of my colleagues kept in contact with me after I left Medtronic. While my close colleagues knew that I left without a job waiting for me, no one reached out to offer support.

My belief that the boss who terminated me also black-listed me was validated shortly after I left Medtronic. To my dismay, he had my picture posted at every security guard station along with the statement "Do Not Let this Person Enter the Facility." A few months later I received an apology from him in a memo circulated widely at Medtronic. But I found this incident extremely hurtful … a feeling that lasted for a few years. Ironically, years later this same ex-boss gave me a very positive, unsolicited recommendation to a prospective consulting client. That got me a substantial amount of consulting work for which I thanked him.

I also worked with him about 10 years later, planning the first Medtronic alumni reunion. Several hundred ex-employees attended it. A lot of war stories were shared that night about our Medtronic experiences.

A few years after I left Medtronic, the person who replaced me as director of clinical research was given a very prestigious award for his accomplishments in that position. Many of them were those I put in place well before being terminated. His name was also substituted for mine in standard operating policies I initiated and in subsequent reprinting of reports I had initially approved. I viewed this award as a validation of my departmental accomplishments.

While a consultant, I attended a presentation Earle Bakken gave to the Twin City medical device community. Earle spoke about Medtronic and what he saw as the future of medicine. He abruptly paused and created a dramatic moment by slowly gazing at each of the fifty or so attendees. Seeing so many familiar faces, Earle sadly remarked that, "I guess we (Medtronic) trained a lot of Twin City professionals." He was absolutely right. I had come to Medtronic as a "diamond in the rough" and left as a polished gem. I left as a highly skilled project manager, technical writer and regulatory and clinical research expert. This expertise served me extremely well in my future professional endeavors.

I took a special watch, awarded to me and a few others, with me when I left Medtronic. Besides displaying the time and my heart rate, it was also a stopwatch. I used it to record billable hours for many years in my consulting practice. I especially enjoyed using it to track the (expensive) billable time I spent on my Medtronic consulting projects. Medtronic was not the only company that terminated me only to hire me back as a consultant. But it was my best client in terms of continued service ... 14 years ... twice as long as the seven years I was a Medtronic employee.

# EPILOGUE

The roller coaster ride continued for many years after I left Medtronic in 1983. Initially I worked for a few years at the Dacomed Corporation, until I was fired for raising concerns about multiple failure modes in the company's new implant. In 1985, I started my own consulting business. I did so to control my own professional fate. For six months, I waited anxiously for any consulting work to materialize. When it did, it came as a huge tidal wave that continued on and on for many years.

Near the end of the twentieth century, I had the distinction of having a client fire me by e-mail. As far as I could tell, I was the first Twin City consultant (or employee) to be fired this way. I wore this distinction proudly then, joking about it often in conversations with family, friends and colleagues.

A few years after my divorce, I married the wonderful woman who proposed to me. She has been a loving wife and my best friend for more than 30 years. We have had many of good times together. We support each other during bad times and there were plenty. We are an ideal couple, except for when we are not.

For almost twelve years, I was the poster child for "How Not to be Semi-Retired." I had to fire myself from three part-time jobs in the last decade to become semi-retired a few months at a time. I truly became semi-retired, just teaching a few university courses yearly, when my last client fired me by e-mail. That ended my 32-year consulting career. Isn't technology great!!!

There are enough stories to fill another book about what I experienced in the second part of my career. I selected four of them to show that my roller coaster ride continued after leaving Medtronic.

# Research Annie

**What I Learned:** *Think carefully about ignoring a boss's directive, no matter how much you disagree with it.*

She came to work a few weeks after I started my new job at Dacomed Corporation in 1983. I was director of clinical and regulatory affairs at Dacomed, a company making erectile dysfunction implants and diagnostic instruments. We dubbed her "Research Annie" to reflect our core business and inject a little good-natured humor into our workplace. At five-foot-eight, impeccably dressed and with bright red hair, she was an imposing presence. She spent most of her time at work, stretched out in one of my office chairs.

Research Annie never objected to the name given her. Those sitting in my office, including me, could easily see that underneath her skirt that she wore no underwear. Rather than being offended by slurs about being a "slut," she flaunted her bright red pubic hair.

On more than one occasion, our president told me to get rid of her. I resisted his directive. To me, it seemed appropriate to have her around. Weren't we a company that designed, manufactured and tested penile implants and erectile dysfunction diagnostics? How could anyone object to having a Research Annie around?

But ultimately, our president prevailed.

So I threw her out!

My wife was very disappointed that I threw her out ... right into trash can. After all, my wife created and meticulously stitched Annie together to be an anatomically correct rag-doll. But there is more to this story.

My 12-year step-daughter saw her mom stitching Research Annie together. Seeing it helped her figure out what I did for a living. And that made her very mad at me. "How can you work on what you do?" she angrily asked several times. Finally, I asked why she was so mad at me.

"Dad, my teacher asked to have all the fathers come to class to tell what they did for a living. I keep telling her that you can't make it. But she keeps asking when you can come to talk to our class."

# Crooked Dick

**What I Learned:** *Something positive can unexpectedly happen at any time, even while being fired.*

About two years later, I was asked to get some pictures of Dacomed's latest penile implant. It consisted of two cylinders, one implanted in each side of the penis. By bending it one way or another, a patient could make his penis assume a flaccid-like appearance or become rigid for intercourse. Implanting it was far less invasive than the surgery required to implant competitive penile prostheses. It was also simpler for patients to use. Both were distinct advantages that marketing wanted to promote. These pictures would be a key part this promotion.

I planned to get the pictures from five Twin City patients who were the first in the nation to get this product. Four patients refused. They were dissatisfied with the rigidity that their implant provided. The fifth one, however, invited me to his home for picture taking.

Just after I arrived at his house and without me asking, he readily stripped down to show me his implant. Its rigid appearance did not look right. "Maybe he did not know how to make it rigid," I thought.

With great reluctance to touch another man's penis, I asked if I could try. Even though I wore latex gloves, I was really uncomfortable holding his penis and maneuvering it. I tried and tried to no avail. While one cylinder worked, the other one was broken. The result was a markedly curved penis that, because of surgical adhesions and his underlying penile disease, was too painful to straighten out.

Naturally, our President asked how the patient's pictures looked.

"His rigid penis is curved substantially to the left, since only one cylinder was working," I replied.

A rigid penis curved substantially is difficult to use for intercourse. Vaginal penetration is typically accomplished with a straight downward thrust. Instead, the vagina has to be approached quite unnaturally using a combined rotating and downward body motion. Of course, this motion could easily be achieved, if a third party was present to operate a navigational-guided winch. So much for intimacy!

After this experience, I wanted to know if this was an isolated failure. I called the other four patients. All four reported rigidity problems, where one or both implanted cylinders remained flaccid.

Dacomed had a serious problem … unexpectedly one that led to me being fired! I was not thanked for independently trying to give attention to this problem and evaluate what caused it. Instead, I was fired for drawing attention to it.

When firing me, the president suggested that I was better suited to be a consultant than an employee. I'm sure I would have just looked for another job, had it not been for this advice. After taking the whole summer off, I took his advice. It led to a great, 32-year consulting career. Dacomed was not so lucky. It subsequently determined that the prosthesis design had serious flaws and had to recall these devices. Since the design flaws were extremely difficult to correct, all production was stopped permanently. A lot of time and money was squandered!

Dacomed subsequently hired me to consult for them for almost two years.

# Leadership

*What I Learned*: *The practice of leadership is both an art and science. Leadership courses and training stress the latter, since the art of leadership relies upon instincts and personal traits.*

Sometime during the mid-1990s, as a consultant for a California company, I was privileged to witness an inspiring example of leadership under fire. I was hired to evaluate their new cardiovascular diagnostic catheter during an open-heart surgery case. That assignment placed me as a guest, mid-late morning in an operating room at the Hennepin County Medical Center.

A mechanical aortic heart valve was being implanted. In this surgery, one side of the valve is sewn inside the heart. Stitches connect the other side of the valve to the aorta, a large artery that carries blood from the heart to almost every other artery in the body.

To evaluate the catheter, I needed to work closely with the anesthesiologist. Therefore, I did not pay much attention to the surgery. But just before the case seemed finished. I heard the surgeon casually mention that one of the stitches had created a small tear in the aorta.

To me, a small tear was merely an interesting wrinkle in an otherwise routine case. Surely a stitch or two would close the tear. I was hungry for lunch and a chance to consult with the anesthesiologist. Surely the case would be over at noon or shortly thereafter. How overly optimistic I was. Stitches used to close that tear created another one. Further stitching created still further tearing. By now, I was engrossed in what was happening. I could see bleeding from the tears. Minutes went by and then an hour. Repairing the torn aorta started to seem hopeless, an exercise in futility.

Meanwhile, the Circulating Nurse and the others in the room started grumbling about the case taking so long. They did not like being in an operating room when never-ending problems were occurring. They also were worried that they might have to continue working there after their shift was over.

As the stitching and tearing continued, the tone of the grumbling changed to a distinctive defeatist attitude. I could hear: "This case is a loser." "He'll never make it out of the operating room."

The surgeon continued, relentlessly trying to close the tears. Eventually, the patient needed blood transfusions to replace the blood lost to bleeding from the torn stitches. A cloud of doom was trying to envelope the entire room, resisted only by the surgeon's undeterred commitment to be successful. If the sky was falling, he was not aware of that

At some point, he must have thought that the staff was more heavily invested in reinforcing their negative feelings about the case than in their support of him and the operation. Something had to be done to reverse the pervasive negativity.

He paused and stepped back a little from the operating table to face the circulating nurse. In a soft-spoken tone, he quietly announced that was going to replace the badly torn part of the aorta with a prosthetic vascular graft. He made it sound like no big deal ... just another day at the office.

"Please get me an aortic graft," he calmly requested. His made that request as though everything was going according to plan. "And by the way, call my wife. Tell her I might not make it home in time for dinner."

His seemingly sarcastic "dinner" comment immediately changed everyone's attitude for the better. The case was successfully concluded within an hour. The nursing staff was able to leave early enough to make the shift change.

I could see that he was a tall man. Otherwise, I did not know anything about this surgeon. I did not know his name nor what he looked like underneath his mask and gown. But I was in awe of the leadership he exhibited that day ... and the mild-mannered way he did it.

# Get Me Two Things

**What I Learned:** *Getting a "Corporate" directive is almost as sacred as quoting biblical scripture.*

One Medtronic manager hired me in the late 1990s as a consultant to help resolve a very interesting challenge. His staff was developing a promising new medical device. Everything was going well, until a corporate regulatory affairs review of their plans. The review's findings brought everything to a screeching halt. Corporate told this manager that a very burdensome, expensive regulatory approach would have to be followed to gain FDA approval to sell this device in the U.S.

This department had no regulatory staff nor did it have sufficient resources to fund additional testing that would be necessary. There were insufficient funds to pay me or another consultant to write the type of FDA submission Corporate wanted.

I did know a way that had a reasonable chance of working. It was a slightly unorthodox approach that I used successfully for clients from smaller companies. Pursing it might be blocked by "Corporate." After all, they had already staked out their position. Usually, only God or some higher power can reverse a corporate decision. Their directive had to be followed.

I explained my proposed approach to this manager. While over-all he liked it, he was concerned about some of the things I said had to be done. There was no problem with me preparing this FDA submission;

consultants were often hired for this purpose. He was concerned with my proposal to send it directly to the FDA. Corporate regulatory affairs would not be told about it until the FDA formally responded to it.

While uncomfortable about going "rogue," he was ultimately willing to accept my advice. He really had no choice. Following Corporate's advice was impossible. And without FDA approval, his promising new medical device was finished as a product. Severe consequences would follow. His willingness to accept my advice was consistent with a common middle management strategy … be successful and then ask for forgiveness afterward, rather than fail by doing nothing.

I asked for and got two things needed to make this scenario work: the title of "Medtronic Consultant" and a new, separate telephone line. Its voicemail message would announce my name and this title. Doing these things were intended to imply that I was an employee and not an independent consultant on voicemail messages or during the conversations that I expected to have with the FDA reviewer about this project.

Corporate regulatory affairs calmly fired me, once they learned what was going on. While they were not pleased, they were not very angry either. Corporate knew I had successfully performed many consulting projects for Medtronic. To them, I was a good guy who briefly went rogue. They also volunteered that my suggested approach had "some" merit.

A few years later, I met a former member of that Department, while consulting at American Medical Systems. "You were right," he said. "We found examples of FDA decisions supporting your approach and discussed them with Corporate. But they still said no."

Unfortunately, I was right about reversing a corporate decision. Perhaps I should have advised them to consult with a higher power before pleading their case with "Corporate."

# ACKNOWLEDGEMENTS

I gratefully acknowledge many people who made my professional career memorable and this book possible.

Stevie Ray inspired me to write this book and provided creative guidance many times along the way. I'm honored to call him "maestro" and friend.

Jeff Howe taught me the practical aspects of bio-medical engineering in surgical and intensive care settings. SciMed owed a lot to him, but never knew it. He was a great colleague and teacher. Jeff is a wonderful human being.

Sheryl Wolk provided valuable editing. More importantly, she helped me make many stories more interesting by including just the right twist at the end.

Several friends, colleagues and acquaintances provided excellent reviews of various versions of the manuscript and/or a sampling of stories. They were: Jennifer Slater, Mike Kaul, Kay Orr, Jeff Roy, Roy Martin, Harvey Vinitsky, Charlotte Lerner, the Sock Monkey Book Club, Dale Stenseth, Gina Risdall and Sherry Bartells. All are thanked for their helpful suggestions, continued support and encouragement of my writing.

Finally, I acknowledge my wife Marsha Wolk. While a skeptic at first, she became my strongest supporter and a great advisor as I labored through the many drafts of this book.

CPSIA information can be obtained
at www.ICGtesting.com
Printed in the USA
FFOW01n1926170418
46295475-47781FF

9 781545 624531